THE GENERAL PROLOGUE TO THE CANTERBURY TALES

BY

GEOFFREY CHAUCER

Edited with Introduction, Notes and Glossary by

JAMES WINNY

CAMBRIDGE
UNIVERSITY PRESS

Published by the Press Syndicate of the University of Cambridge
The Pitt Building, Trumpington Street, Cambridge CB2 1RP
40 West 20th Street, New York, NY 10011–4211, USA
10 Stamford Road, Oakleigh, Melbourne 3166, Australia

ISBN 0 521 04629 7 821. 1 CHA

First published 1966
Twenty-sixth printing 1995

Printed in Great Britain at the
University Press, Cambridge

for my son

DANIEL

CONTENTS

Note on the Frontispiece

The figure shown in the frontispiece, taken from a misericord in the parish church of St Lawrence at Ludlow, probably represents a warden of the local Gild of Palmers. He is depicted wearing costume of the late fourteenth century and a chain of office. His figure and expression suggest the commanding human qualities which Chaucer attributes to many of his pilgrims—especially to the Host, Harry Bailly.

ACKNOWLEDGEMENT

This edition has benefited from criticism offered by several colleagues associated with the production of the Cambridge Chaucer, and from the assistance of the editorial staff of the Cambridge University Press.

J. W.

CAMBRIDGE
April 1964

INTRODUCTION

The date of Geoffrey Chaucer's birth is not known. He died in 1400, a few years short of sixty, having lived during the reigns of three English kings: Edward III, Richard II and Henry IV. The poet was probably well known to each of them. His career as a courtier began early in his life, when he became page to Prince Lionel, a son of Edward III, and it continued up to his death. As a young man he served with the king's army in France, where he was captured and ransomed; and later in life he was several times employed on diplomatic missions abroad. Marks of royal favour are expressed in the pensions and gifts which Chaucer received from each of his three sovereigns. His competence as a man of affairs is attested by a series of civil appointments; as a senior customs official, then as Clerk of the King's Works, and as parliamentary representative for his own county of Kent.[1] His career as a poet was evidently secondary to his activities as courtier and civil servant, which must have absorbed much of Chaucer's time and energy. Official records contain no reference to his literary work. No doubt the court knew him as a poet. One of the earliest of Chaucer's poems which has survived, *The Book of the Duchess*, seems to have been written as an expression of John of Gaunt's grief at the death of his first wife, Blanche, in 1369; and tradition asserts that *The Legend of Good Women* was written at the request of Richard II's wife, Queen Anne, to whom the poem is dedicated. How

---

[1] Chaucer's life as courtier and public official is described in greater detail in *An Introduction to Chaucer*, ch. 5.

far Chaucer was known as a poet outside court circles is uncertain. The reputation of a medieval writer was largely dependent upon the copying and transmission of manuscripts, which was a notoriously slow and expensive business. If one of Chaucer's own characters can be taken seriously, his fame had spread to the common people; for this pilgrim complains that Chaucer has made it difficult for anyone to tell a story by relating them all himself:

> And if he have noght seyd hem, leve brother,
> In o book, he hath seyd hem in another.

The poet's mockery of himself seems to contain an admission that his literary reputation has carried well beyond the court.

This reputation has held firm for nearly six centuries, commanding respect from poet and critic in every succeeding age, despite changes of language and fluctuations of literary taste. The Chaucer of secret missions and public affairs left no mark on history, but the poet continues to hold an audience; most decisively by the culminating work of his life, *The Canterbury Tales*. At the simplest assessment, this is a collection of twenty-four stories in verse and prose, some incomplete, told as entertainment by a group of pilgrims riding from London to the shrine of Thomas à Becket at Canterbury. In the *General Prologue* to these tales Chaucer, himself one of the pilgrims, explains how the proposal for a story-telling competition was made after supper at the Tabard Inn, before the pilgrimage set out, and gives a personal description of the 'nine-and-twenty' men and women who are to be his companions on the road.[1] The individual tales which follow are given

[1] Chaucer actually enumerates thirty pilgrims in the original company. The addition of himself and the Host brings the total to

continuity by a series of narrative links which join heads and tails together. Some of these links are missing, and in consequence the poem as it stands consists of nine fragments, the longest run of continuous narrative containing six tales. There are other signs that Chaucer did not complete the great work which he had designed. The original plan proposed by the Host required each of the thirty pilgrims to relate four tales, two on the outward journey and two during the return to London. Somewhere between Southwark and Canterbury this ambitious plan is silently dropped, for the Host later speaks as though he had demanded only one tale from each pilgrim. Even this modified plan is not carried out, for on a final tally there are twenty complete tales and four which are interrupted or which break off abruptly. But despite the gaps and anomalies which reveal the unfinished state of the whole poem, *The Canterbury Tales* has the coherence and imaginative drive of a great work of literature, and presents a firmly realized view of life.

Of all medieval poems, *The Canterbury Tales* gives a modern reader the strongest sense of contact with the life and manners of fourteenth-century England. The group of pilgrims whom Chaucer joins at Southwark does not provide a complete cross-section of contemporary English society, but many of the missing figures of the aristocracy and lower classes are supplied in the tales, which seem to include references to every aspect of domestic life. Their background of inns, farm-yards, city streets and middle-class houses has a range and variety that only Shakespeare

thirty-two, which is further increased when the Canon's Yeoman joins the pilgrimage. But Chaucer's miscount has acquired the force of a tradition which most commentators respect.

was to surpass, and their human figures have a similar rich diversity. From the benches and jugs of the artisan household to the fishponds and walled gardens of the affluent, Chaucer seems to have represented the whole texture of medieval life—its sounds and colours, its characteristic tastes and its idioms of common speech. In the *General Prologue* the original nine-and-twenty are subjected to an affectionately close scrutiny which makes us see, behind the flamboyant dress and striking personal features of these strongly individual men and women, the social and economic pressures which have shaped them. Their abundant vitality and self-assurance suggest a society whose growing wealth was encouraging the middle classes to assert themselves vigorously. The Wife of Bath's scarlet stockings and the Merchant's beaver hat throw light on the personality of each, but also hint at the bold manners and expensive tastes which commercial prosperity was fostering.

The materialistic outlook of the times is repeatedly disclosed in the *General Prologue*. The hypocritical Friar, who has no dealings with the sick and the needy, 'but al with riche and selleres of vitaille', and the Physician who 'lovede gold in special' for its medicinal qualities, typify the greed and acquisitiveness of most of their fellows. The Merchant is forever talking about his business profits, but supplements his income by trafficking in foreign currency. The Miller defrauds his customers by stealing part of the corn which he grinds, and the Shipman mixes piracy and theft with his lawful affairs at sea. Chaucer is not exclusively concerned with the world of medieval trade and finance. The Clerk's threadbare pursuit of knowledge, and the Physician's familiar acquaintance with 'olde Esculapius', Hippocrates, Galen and a dozen other medical authorities, represent the state of medieval learning. The fastidious table-manners of the Prioress illustrate the standards of polite behaviour adopted by the upper classes, with whom she is trying to identify herself. The Franklin's sumptuous meals of partridge and bream, the Cook's special dish of chicken boiled with marrow-bones and spices, and the taste for garlic, onions and leeks which confirms the Summoner's coarseness, outline the character of medieval food and cookery. The side-arms carried by several of the pilgrims remind us how far the medieval traveller had to depend upon himself to safeguard his life and property. Finally, the presence of eight ecclesiastical figures[1] in a mixed group of thirty pilgrims indicates the extent to which medieval life was dominated by the power of the Church.

Through his description of these eight pilgrims, Chaucer makes us see how increasing wealth and authority have weakened the previously austere discipline of the Church and corrupted its moral values. Of this group of supposedly dedicated men and women, only the Parson— in social status and appearance the least distinguished of them—remains true to the ideals of his vocation. He accepts poverty and the endless duties of a scattered country parish, and ignores the insidious appeal of a comfortable, well-paid appointment as a chantry priest in London. The others have succumbed to the attractions of the world of social affairs. The pleasure-loving Monk declares an open disdain for the 'olde thinges' which

[1] Monk, Friar, Nun's Priest, Parson, Summoner, Pardoner, Prioress and Second Nun. The Summoner is not in holy orders, but is an officer of the Church. Of the 'preestes thre' mentioned in line 164 only one can be taken seriously—the narrator of the *Nun's Priest's Tale*.

embody the principles of his monastic order, and argues earnestly and with no sense of anomaly against the restrictions of the cloistered life. The attempts of the Prioress to 'countrefete cheere of court' without regard to her religious vows show how the same worldly outlook has permeated another former stronghold of asceticism. The Pardoner is a blatant and self-confessed example of the greed which he preaches against, and the Friar cultivates the society of the rich and the well-provisioned, giving them absolution on a simple monetary basis—selling, in effect, one of the sacraments of the Church. Although the Parson and the Knight make a stand against the materialism of the age by following a selfless ideal, the main impression of medieval society left by the *General Prologue* is of its frankly acquisitive purpose. The Church has capitulated to the power of money, leaving society to enrich itself without too scrupulous a regard for moral principle.

The worldliness of contemporary outlook and the declining spiritual authority of the Church are evident in the pilgrimage itself. The four-day journey to Canterbury offers the pilgrims opportunities of self-examination and meditation before they reach the shrine of the martyred archbishop, but they show no inclination to take the occasion seriously. Instead, they regard the pilgrimage as a holiday excursion and a release for their high spirits, finding nothing incongruous in the Host's suggestion of a story-telling competition to relieve the tedium of the journey. Chaucer himself arrives at the Tabard 'with ful devout corage'; but the opening lines of the *General Prologue* give an ironic indication of the way religious pilgrimages had come to be treated. Their association with the re-awakening of the earth in springtime suggests that the impulse to visit a distant shrine springs from the same natural prompting. The Wife of Bath, irrepressibly convivial and promiscuous, is an enthusiastic devotee of pilgrimages who has made the long and hazardous journey to Jerusalem three times, apart from visiting the most famous European shrines. Her enthusiasm suggests the kind of entertainment which she expected of a pilgrimage; and perhaps Chaucer's remark that she 'koude muchel of wandringe by the weye' implies that curiosity, rather than devotion, was the driving force of these expeditions abroad. From the rambling prologue to her tale it might seem that the Wife had joined the pilgrimage to Canterbury in the hope of finding a sixth husband. Not many of the pilgrims seem to have any better reason for undertaking the journey than to enjoy the inviting weather and a few days of good fellowship.

The pilgrimage is primarily a device by which Chaucer brings together a group of otherwise unconnected stories, ranging in literary type from the broad fabliau to the courtly romance, and including religious legend, moral exemplum, fairy-tale and other kinds of narrative. The diversity of the tales—some of them dating from an earlier period of Chaucer's life—raised the problem of binding together stories of widely differing character. The difficulty was brilliantly overcome by the device of a pilgrimage, which brings together story-tellers of strongly individual tastes and contrasting social backgrounds. It followed from this plan that the story-tellers would not be mere mouthpieces, but fully realized figures with an importance of their own, and that their stories would be to some extent a reflexion of personal character. Towards the end of the *General Prologue* Chaucer draws attention to this point by apologizing in advance for any indelicate expressions used by the pilgrims, which his own narrative must repeat. As he explains,

> Whoso shal telle a tale after a man,
> He moot reherce as ny as evere he kan
> Everich a word, if it be in his charge,
> Al speke he never so rudeliche and large. (733–6)

The joke of shifting responsibility to his own characters has its serious side, for it shows Chaucer's intention of giving his pilgrims lifelike individuality, through forms of speech appropriate to their rank and personal temperament. Without going so far as to write the tales in regional dialects or the vulgar language of churls and villeins, Chaucer does indicate the character of the speaker through his idiom. The pilgrims are more comprehensively revealed by their individual choice of tale.

The relationship of story-teller with his tale is not to be pressed too far. While Chaucer arranges some very happy marriages of this kind, other associations seem either arbitrary or directed by convenience. We can suppose that the tales which Chaucer wrote after the *General Prologue* were shaped to fit particular characters whom he had now described. *The Pardoner's Tale*, a story of greed and treachery leading to violent death, provides a deeply ironic commentary on the Pardoner himself which would lose much of its point if separated from its teller. The Wife of Bath's prologue to her tale, twice as long as the tale itself, is a shameless account of her marital adventures which develops the lively portrait drawn in the *General Prologue*. The farcical indecencies of *The Miller's Tale* illuminate Chaucer's description of a pilgrim whose talk was 'moost of sinne and harlotries'. In each of these cases the tale sends us back to the graphic sketch of character in the *General Prologue* with sharpened appreciation of its discernment. On the other hand, the tales written before the unifying design of a pilgrimage had occurred to Chaucer do not have this sense of belonging to their tellers. *The Knight's Tale* has some nominal connexion with the chivalrous code of behaviour which the Knight observes, but his romance of Palamon and Arcite is not altogether the story which might have been expected of a fighting-man of many campaigns. The Man of Law's tale from folklore has no bearing upon his character as the *General Prologue* sardonically draws it, and when the jolly fox-hunting Monk offers a dreary recital of tragedies, 'of which I have an hundred in my celle', we must share the exasperation which eventually produces an angry protest from the Knight.

The Monk's Tale, written in the stanzaic form which Chaucer had used in *Troilus and Criseyde* and *The Parliament of Fowls*, probably belongs with them to the middle period of his literary career. The Monk hardly deserves to be saddled with so gloomy and introspective a tale, but with limited time at his disposal Chaucer could not afford to discard the story altogether. With the ingenuity of a great artist, he made capital out of its very deficiency of 'mirthe and solaas', bringing the tale into the collection so that it could be sacrificed to provide a dramatic moment in the pilgrimage. This example of conscious mismatching between tale and teller should warn us not to look for a close relationship between every pilgrim and his story. Several tales have been fitted into the grand design without much adaptation or revision. The Knight's remark during his narrative, 'But of that storie list me nat to write' (line

1201), has been allowed to stand unrevised. Some of the tales have evidently been shuffled into alternative positions which may remain tentative. The narrator of *The Shipman's Tale* refers to himself as a woman, and since this is not a story which a nun could have repeated in public, it may originally have been ascribed to the Wife of Bath and transferred to the Shipman when a more suitable wifely tale was found. The Second Nun reveals another change of purpose by speaking of herself as a 'son of Eve'.

For these reasons we cannot always expect a subtly illuminating relationship between a tale and its narrator. Chaucer's task was to match tales and pilgrims as closely as possible, but the range of narrative forms was much more restricted than the permutations of human character, and places had to be found for tales written without particular regard to the temperament or profession of the narrator. In general, it is enough if the matching is not obviously inappropriate. The pilgrims do not exist merely as mouthpieces for Chaucer's tales. They have a life that is independent of their narrative function, as actors in a seemingly undirected comedy of human behaviour and emotions through which Chaucer expresses part of his outlook as poet. The men and women whose portraits the *General Prologue* presents are not described simply because Chaucer has tales for them to tell. Several of them, among them the Yeoman and the Plowman, are never called upon; and the Nun's Priest who tells one of the most appealing stories is unaccountably passed over in Chaucer's introduction of the company. His needle-sharp impressions of personality, caught by a discerning eye and set down with such sly appreciation of human weakness, prove Chaucer deeply absorbed in the human figures which the Canterbury pilgrimage assembles. In solving the problem of binding together such diverse and unrelated stories, Chaucer also found the means of expressing his sense of the turbulent vitality of human beings and affairs.

The twenty-one full-length descriptions of men and women which the *General Prologue* contains[1] take up about three-quarters of the poem. The length of these individual portraits varies considerably. The Cook is rapidly disposed of in nine lines and the Merchant in fifteen, but the account of the Prioress runs to forty-five lines, and of the Summoner to forty-six. The most extended description—that of the Friar—is over four times as long as the graphic picture of the Yeoman. This unequal treatment suggests Chaucer's eye lingering upon the more intriguingly complex of the pilgrims, whose individuality could not be summed up in a few revealing images. He usually spends least time upon the pilgrims low in the social scale, epitomizing their character through some telling physical feature, such as the Shipman's half-concealed dagger. The technique of description varies as much as the degree of detail which Chaucer supplies. Dress, physical appearance and personal habits provide the most immediate index of individual character. The Yeoman is concretely realized in the phrase, 'a not heed with a broun visage', which besides suggesting the weather-beaten toughness of the man implies his enduring loyalty of service. The depraved moral nature of the Summoner is revealed by the disfiguring lumps in a burning red face which makes him a terror to children. A single note on the

[1] The five Gildsmen are summarily described as a group, and the Second Nun and the anomalous 'preestes thre' are mentioned only as being present.

Wife of Bath's costume, 'a foot-mantel aboute hir hipes large', brings her before us in the incorrigible reality of flesh which dominates her existence, as the 'spores sharpe' on her feet betray her love of mastery. The indolent Monk shows his taste for comfort and luxury by his fur-trimmed sleeves and supple boots; and the over-fastidious manners of the Prioress—the only pilgrim whose behaviour at table Chaucer thinks it worth commenting upon—disclose a woman straining to acquire the delicate sensibility of a lady, but betraying her social background by the accent of her cockney French.

These direct allusions to personality are sometimes re-inforced by an account of the pilgrim's past experience and professional standing. The portrait of the Knight consists largely of a detailed list of the crusading wars in which he has spent most of his life: a record of self-abnegation for which Chaucer shows respect by saying little about the Knight's personal appearance. The Parson is presented in a similar fashion. Unlike the less virtuous pilgrims, who are given flesh-and-blood solidity through characteristic features of dress or personal mannerisms, the Parson remains an impression without clear form. The picture of him visiting his flock, 'upon his feet, and in his hand a staf', suggests his Christian humility rather than his physical appearance, and the long de-scription of his pastoral activities which occupies most of the portrait says nothing about his domestic background, which seems non-existent. The Man of Law and the Phy-sician, like the Knight, are described rather in terms of their professional qualifications and practice than through such personal features as the Wife's 'gat-tothed' mouth or the Miller's bristly wart. But here a subtly ironic observation is at work, penetrating the self-important disguise of the professional man and exposing the human reality beneath. The legal expertise of the Man of Law, to whom 'al was fee simple in effect', is commended in a double-edged phrase which implies that he pocketed his client's money without exerting himself very strenuously. The Physician is praised as a 'verray, parfit praktisour'; a claim which Chaucer supports by an impressive list of the medical authorities whose works this pilgrim has studied. It is only after three lines of comment upon the Physician's cautious diet that Chaucer adds, as though by way of irrelevant afterthought, that 'his studie was but litel on the Bible'.

Whatever Chaucer's private moral standards, he appears to regard the moral failings of the pilgrims with an amiable indulgence at times bordering on approval. He observes the Wife's huge appetite for experience as though with admiration, admitting the irregularity of her younger days only to remark that 'therof nedeth nat to speke as nowthe'; and goes so far as to agree with the Monk's scandalous argument that the world must be served. But this attitude conceals a comic irony that cannot deceive us for long. Exposure of moral weakness is most effective when it springs unconsciously from the man's own behaviour, and Chaucer's subtlest technique of character description is to allow the pilgrim to expatiate upon his own beliefs and accomplishments. Both the Monk and the Friar are presented partly through their own reported speech:

> What sholde he studie and make himselven wood,
> Upon a book in cloistre alwey to poure,
> Or swinken with his handes, and laboure,
> As Austin bit? How shal the world be served?
> Lat Austin have his swink to him reserved! (184–8)

The energetic tone of the argument makes it seem that Chaucer supports the Monk's opinion, where in fact he is repeating the substance of the Monk's appeal to reason sardonically, aware that his proposal makes nonsense of his religious vocation. The Monk is asking, in effect, for a monastic life indistinguishable from the existence of a wealthy landowner such as the Franklin, with no religious duties or restrictions upon personal enjoyment. The absurdity of the suggestion, although not recognized by the Monk, does not require any comment from Chaucer. Nor does he need to express an opinion of the Friar, a cynical moral impostor who is made to condemn himself by his contempt for the poor and the sick:

> For unto swich a worthy man as he
> Acorded nat, as by his facultee,
> To have with sike lazars aqueyntaunce.
> It is nat honest, it may nat avaunce,
> For to deelen with no swich poraille,
> But al with riche and selleres of vitaille.   (243–8)

Again Chaucer reports the argument verbatim, as though impressed by its soundness and good sense. But the phrase, 'swich a worthy man as he', reveals his sarcasm, and the stinging disdain of the Friar's reference to the poor, 'no swich poraille', reveals not his lordly superiority but the hard, grasping covetousness of his inner nature.

As the pilgrimage and the story-telling get under way, the pilgrims begin to disclose themselves more intimately. In the *General Prologue* they are frozen into characteristic attitudes and isolated from one another, as though to prevent their charged individualities from colliding. The pilgrimage releases them from these formal poses and allows them to express themselves through action— arguing, applauding, interrupting, quarrelling over precedence, but above all talking. The head-and-tail links prove Chaucer's remarkable talent as a writer of racy vernacular dialogue which seems to catch the accent of popular medieval speech. The cautiously roundabout remarks of the Host leading up to the proposal of a story-telling contest—affable, expansive, yet walking on tiptoe—provide the first indication of the gift which Chaucer will display more conspicuously in the pilgrims' conversation on the road. The long preamble to *The Wife of Bath's Tale* is his most sustained achievement of this kind. The Wife's steady flow of highly personal reminiscence, which defies interruption and falters only when she momentarily loses the thread of her story, does more than reveal a dubious moral character. Her choice of words and turn of phrase let us see personality impressing itself upon the raw materials of language, to form a dramatic image of her own pulsing vitality:

> But, Lord Crist! whan that it remembreth me
> Upon my yowthe, and on my jolitee,
> It tikleth me aboute myn herte roote.
> Unto this day it dooth myn herte boote
> That I have had my world as in my time.

The Reeve looks back on his experience in the prologue to his tale, but without the joyous sense of triumph which carries the Wife through more than eight hundred lines of monologue:

> But ik am oold, me list not pley for age;
> Gras time is doon, my fodder is now forage;
> This white top writeth mine olde yeris;
> Myn herte is also mowled[1] as mine heris.

The verse moves stiffly, and is end-stopped as though to represent the physical awkwardness of an old man, whose

[1] *mowled*, decayed.

spirit has dried up with his body. The two passages illustrate briefly how Chaucer matches the voice to the pilgrim, confirming the initial impression of character in the *General Prologue* through an idiom of speech which sets the individual moving.

Whichever technique of description Chaucer uses, his portrait realizes personal character as an immediately tangible presence, as though each of the pilgrims had an individual shape and texture as distinctive as the creatures of a medieval Noah's ark. The pilgrims can be fitted into various contemporary categories, as that of physiological type which identifies the Franklin as sanguine and the Reeve as choleric, but no classification is ample enough to account for all the varieties of human personality which the portraits describe. By displaying an almost unlimited diversity of private attributes, through style of dress, behaviour, physiognomy, age, moral character or idiom of speech, the pilgrims convey Chaucer's sense of the tireless outpouring of inventive genius which sustains natural life. The hauteur of the Merchant, the patient absorption of the Clerk and the Monk's beaming *joie de vivre* are qualities as uniquely distinctive as the hideousness of the Summoner and the unclouded gaiety of the Squire. Each represents a fresh and original variation on the theme of common man, through which Chaucer pays an imaginative tribute to the still greater creative capacity of nature.

This does not mean that Chaucer sees his company of pilgrims simply as an incongruous assortment of pantomime figures, to be enjoyed for their grotesquely comic oddity. The pervasive element of social satire in the *General Prologue*—most prominent in his account of the ecclesiastical figures—suggests Chaucer's serious concern at the debasing of moral standards, and at the materialistic outlook which had taken hold of society. There are moments, as when he records the Friar's sneering contempt for the poor, which seem to show Chaucer's habitual good temper revolting against the cynical opportunism which had become widespread in ecclesiastical life. Such moments are rare and uncharacteristic of Chaucer. His usual attitude towards the moral weakness which he discloses is one of mocking amusement; not so much at man's often ludicrous shortcomings as at their incompatibility with the picture of himself which he presents to the world. The Shipman is a thievish pirate, the Reeve a cunning embezzler, the Physician has a dishonest private understanding with his druggist, and the Man of Law 'semed bisier than he was'. The efforts of the Prioress to mimic courtly manners are detected and set down with the same intuitive sense of false appearance as allows Chaucer to penetrate the Merchant's imposing disguise. The mask of respectability is not roughly torn off, for while he is describing his pilgrims Chaucer is maintaining an outward manner that is awed and deferential; telling us that the Prioress was 'of greet desport', that the Monk was a manly man, 'to been an abbot able', or that the murderous Shipman was an incomparable navigator and pilot. Because he does not insist upon their moral failings or hypocritical manner, revealing them with an ironic innocence of manner and leaving them to speak for themselves, Chaucer's approach to his pilgrims suggests a psychologist rather than a moralist. He presents vices and shortcomings within the context of human individuality, as a product of the curious pressures which stamp a unique personality upon each of the pilgrims. The Shipman's easy conscience is an integral part of the tough, self-reliant spirit of the man, which has acquired the wilfulness and moral unconcern of the elements in which he lives. His thefts and murders, the Franklin's epicurism, the Physician's avarice, interest Chaucer not as evidence of a breakdown of moral values but for what they reveal of individual character.

Thus Chaucer's satire is not directed against contemporary morals, but against the comic self-ignorance which gives man two identities—the creature he is, and the more distinguished and inscrutable person he imagines himself to be. As critical analyst of the pilgrims' appearance and manners, Chaucer stands a little apart from the compact group of nine-and-twenty, accepted as a fellow-pilgrim yet not entirely of their company. The much sharper awareness which allows him to seize upon the crucial features of each individual separates him from them, as a detached observer who cannot share their absorbed interest in external events. Characteristically, he does not attempt to make capital out of his commanding position. Instead, throughout *The Canterbury Tales* Chaucer depicts himself as a shyly inconspicuous person, overawed by the impressive company to which he has attached himself, and struggling to rise above his sense of inferiority. The Host recognizes this timidity in Chaucer, and when he calls the poet forward to begin his tale describes him with condescending amusement as 'elvissh by his contenaunce', remarking disrespectfully that this would be 'a popet in an arm t'enbrace for any womman'. Chaucer is anxious to please despite this mockery, but he can only offer a rhyming tale 'lerned longe agoon'; a puerile romance which the Host soon brings to an end with some painfully blunt criticism. More out of pity than respect he is allowed to start again, this time with 'a litel thing in prose' which goes on interminably, to the Host's not very discriminating satisfaction.

This ironic presentation of himself as an incapable dreamer is anticipated in the *General Prologue*, where Chaucer ignores himself almost completely. What we know of his career as courtier, ambassador and civil servant, and of his cosmopolitan experience, makes the reticence of the bare phrase 'and myself' itself seem ironic; but the Chaucer of the poems is clearly not the Chaucer of public life. In his writing he assumes the conventional character of poet, making himself appear vague and impractical; too deeply immersed in fantasy to deal effectively with the business of material life. A shy, half-apologetic figure among the flesh and blood and more volatile spirits of the other pilgrims, he seems wistfully envious of their self-confident capability, as though these were qualities which he could not hope to possess. But Chaucer has his tongue in his cheek. His innocent simplicity of manner masks the discernment of a commentator better acquainted with the everyday world, and in particular with the foibles of human character, than any of the pilgrims who overshadow him. Like his pretence of literary ignorance and of uncommunicative shyness, Chaucer's simplicity is a comic disguise. He joins the pilgrimage ostensibly as its one undistinguished member, awkwardly out of his depth among so many eminent and forceful personalities, but in reality as the one observer who cannot be deceived by an impressive outward appearance, or by the unconscious dissimulation which is much harder to detect. The Host makes a joke of his self-effacing modesty:

> Thou lookest as thou woldest finde an hare,
> For evere upon the ground I se thee stare.

But the laugh is against the Host. The man who noticed the inscription on the Prioress's brooch and the vernicle sewed into the Pardoner's cap missed very little.

The comic irony of his self-portraiture must have been more obvious to Chaucer's immediate audience, who knew him as he was. A modern reader may be initially taken in by his straight-faced innocence of manner. His impressions of costume, complexion and personal habits in the *General Prologue* read like random notes on character whose occasionally damaging disclosures arise accidentally and without Chaucer's notice. 'She was a worthy womman al hir live,' he remarks admiringly of the Wife, adding as though to support his judgement, 'Housbondes at chirche dore she hadde five.' For a moment the tone of the remark may deceive us. Both its unhurried timing and the conversational blandness of the comment suggest that Chaucer is merely developing his argument. It needs a second look to recognize the incongruity of the two remarks, and to appreciate the ironic purpose which has set them together. We may be similarly misled by Chaucer's approving judgement of the Monk's scandalous argument. 'I seyde his opinioun was good', is too condensed a comment to show whether or not Chaucer was being sarcastic. It suggests most immediately that, under the influence of the Monk's commanding personality, Chaucer found the logic of his complaint impressive. When we know him better, we see the comic irony of his

Introduction

reply, but meanwhile the artless pilgrim whom Chaucer puts into the story under his own name continues to act as decoy.

In *The Canterbury Tales* Chaucer assumes a double identity. The observer who travels with the pilgrims, dazed by their ebullience and unable to offer a comparable tale, is a comically inverted form of Chaucer's real self whose incompetence adds to the fun of the story. By presenting his characters through the eyes of his impressionable counterpart, who seems not always to realize the ironic significance of his own remarks, Chaucer achieves a satirical effect whose innocent tone makes the disclosure more telling. The pilgrim narrator misses the point, and yet it is made unmistakably. The actual discernment and organizing power which Chaucer disclaims through his comic mouthpiece appear in the work itself. The author stands apart from his poem, amusedly watching his pilgrim self being carried along like a straw by the great wave of human energy which Chaucer has himself set in motion. Immersed in the events of the pilgrimage, and entirely subservient to the authority of the Host, the Chaucer of *The Canterbury Tales* seems completely out of his depth. Paradoxically, this pretence of helplessness serves to underline Chaucer's critical direction of the whole poem. His readiness to treat himself with playful disrespect, as a background figure incapable of affecting the course of events, conceals the relaxed and confident outlook of a poet whose work falls entirely within his shaping control. In more than one sense the author is watching his own performance. By putting a workaday version of himself among the pilgrims, to be scrutinized by the Host with the same unsparing directness as he has turned upon the original nine-and-twenty, Chaucer suggests how deeply the poem is invigorated by his critical self-awareness. Everywhere, though unobtrusively, he is in charge.

Like Chaucer, the Host is not one of the original company. Although he introduces the poet unceremoniously as a figure of fun, on his side Chaucer describes the Host respectfully as a proper man,

> For to han been a marchal in an halle.　　(754)

The pilgrims acknowledge his superior judgement and natural gifts of leadership with the same deference. It says enough for his force of character that when the Host proposes the story-telling competition, offering himself as master of ceremonies and critical arbiter, the company of forceful and distinguished individuals think it best not to deliberate over his suggestion, and agree to be 'reuled at his devys'. The Host's skilful handling of the various crises which arise during the journey proves the wisdom of their decision. Whatever threatens to disorder the company and frustrate his sociable purpose—arguments over precedence, drunkenness, a boring tale, bad blood between professional rivals, or the Pardoner's sinister attempt to usurp the leadership—finds the Host alert and primed for action, with means varying between mild badinage and an invective which leaves its victim speechless with rage and shame. His individual approach to the pilgrims reveals an experienced judgement of men, and an instinctive gift of fitting words to the occasion. His proposal to the company after supper has an expansive *bonhomie* that is tempered on the following morning, when he reminds the pilgrims of their undertaking, and softened again when, satisfied of their purpose, he calls

forward the Knight with the politeness due to his social
rank:

> 'Sire Knight,' quod he, 'my maister and my lord,
> Now draweth cut, for that is myn accord.'   (839–40)

His invitation to the Prioress has the engaging delicacy
and hesitation of a wooer which even this scrupulously
mannered *grande dame* of the suburbs finds irresistible:

> My lady Prioresse, by youre leve,
> So that I wiste I sholde yow nat greve,
> I wolde demen that ye tellen sholde
> A tale next, if so were that ye wolde.
> Now wol ye vouche sauf, my lady deere?

But he calls up the Clerk with the disdainful suspicion of
an illiterate man of the world towards a scholarly recluse,
telling him roughly not to perplex his audience with the
complications of high style but to deliver himself in plain
vernacular terms. 'Speketh so pleyn at this time, we yow
preye,' he asks, with an edge of sarcasm in his politeness,
'That we may understonde what ye seye.' When he gives
way to the Miller's drunken insistence, recognizing the
pointlessness of wasting reasonable breath upon a sot, his
manner drops abruptly to a scornful curtness of expression:

> Tel on, a devel way!
> Thou art a fool; thy wit is overcome.

His critical judgement of literature is usually expressed in
the same abrupt and unequivocal fashion. He interrupts
Chaucer's disappointing tale of Sir Thopas with a roar of
exasperation, and delivers himself of his opinions with a
vehemence that ignores the normal courtesies, and even
the decencies, of polite conversation:

'Mine eres aken of thy drasty[1] speche:
Now swich a rym the devel I biteche![2]
This may wel be rym dogerel,' quod he.

Yet he can also be generously admiring in his praise, as he shows by his appreciative comments on the Nun's Priest's tale, and deeply moved by pathos. Changing his manner at every fresh turn of events, the Host maintains his position as leader of the company without serious difficulty; though the task of keeping the competition moving forward against checks and diversions makes constant demands upon his ingenuity and strength of purpose. As he gathers the pilgrims into a submissive flock on the first morning, so by diplomacy, good humour or sheer force of will he continues to hold them together as a body; cajoling, rebuking, bantering and sometimes grossly insulting individual pilgrims who bring the general harmony of the company into hazard. Of all the pilgrims, he offers the fullest contrast to the inoffensive reserve of Chaucer: an accomplished master of men, able to command by right of his natural authority and his instinctive judgement of character.

Although he and Chaucer represent opposite extremes of temperament, the two men share some significant points of likeness. It is the Host who suggests the story-telling game, who determines the order in which the tales are related, and who cuts off tedious or depressing stories which try his patience too far.[3] It is also he, as we have

---

[1] *drasty*, worthless.   [2] *biteche*, commit to.

[3] In point of fact it is the Franklin who brings the Squire's tale to an end with kindly commendation, and the Knight who first interrupts the Monk's tragic recital. But the Host acts as general arbiter and critic throughout, in accordance with the agreement made at line 817 of the *General Prologue*.

just seen, who preserves order when unruly or rebellious feelings break out among the pilgrims. In all these respects the Host acts as though on his author's behalf, or as a front for Chaucer's manipulation of events. The idea of a story-telling competition springs of course from Chaucer, and not from the Host, just as it is Chaucer who actually decides in what order the story-tellers make their appearance. For reasons which he may not have consciously worked out, Chaucer transferred his own authority as puppet-master to one of his own characters, and invested the Host with the robust human qualities which he ironically denied to his own timid counterpart in the story. The two figures—one comprehensively assured, the other nervous and bashful—are related within the author of *The Canterbury Tales*, as positive and negative aspects of the same blended personality. As organizer and director of the whole venture, the Host takes over Chaucer's literary function, while, as though to distract attention from his substitute's activities, Chaucer admits himself to the pilgrimage, as a minnow among the tritons. What can be inferred of Geoffrey Chaucer's capacities, as a public servant entrusted with responsible duties, and the discernment and experience which have gone into the portraits of the *General Prologue*, encourage us to suppose that the actual Chaucer had rather more in common with the Host than with his slightly ludicrous namesake in *The Canterbury Tales*. But Chaucer was a poet as well as Clerk of the King's Works.

So far as Chaucer can be identified with any of the characters of the *General Prologue*, he must appear to some degree in each of them; for the poetic vision of human life which represents him most completely is expressed through all the figures which he has created. Nonetheless, we may still recognize that the Host has qualities which give him a special significance in the design of *The Canterbury Tales*. Apart from directing its whole action as puppet-master, he prevents the company from breaking apart as clashes of temperament produce a series of emotional crises. Without him to repress these sudden eruptions of energy as the pilgrims elbow their way to the front or attack one another in flurries of childish anger, the company would disintegrate. Its human elements are too diverse to cohere except under powerful pressure, and only the commanding personality of the Host can bind its volatile substance into a unified body. Elizabethan readers might have seen the Host as the figure of reason subduing the rebellious impulses of man's physical nature; but if any unconscious allegory is present it relates to the activity of the poet, and not of the moralist. Chaucer seems to be representing through the pilgrims a state of imaginative turbulence, an outpouring of creative energy, which can only be directed by the masterful purpose which the Host embodies.

This interpretation is useful if it draws attention to the characteristic vigour of Chaucer's writing; a feature of his literary style which shows most conspicuously in his insistently emphatic manner. None of the pilgrims is allowed to be less than exceptional. The Man of Law is 'ful riche of excellence', the Friar 'the beste beggere in his hous'. Of the Shipman Chaucer declares 'ther nas noon swich from Hulle to Cartage', and similarly of the Doctor of Physic, 'in al this world ne was ther noon him lik'. In her cloth-making the Wife of Bath 'passed hem of Ypres and of Gaunt', showing the same professional expertise as the Yeoman, who knew woodcraft inside and out, and the Reeve whom no auditor could catch out in his farm accounts. The 'verray, parfit gentil knight' who heads the company sets the standard for all the other pilgrims, who display the same super-eminence of professional or human character, whatever their social degree. The Host's compliment to the pilgrims, that so distinguished a company was never under his roof before, seems to understate the facts badly. Such a collection of men and women could exist only in the imagination of a poet who saw life with a heightened awareness of its material reality, and created a poetic image of this private experience. The concentrating and intensifying of physical sensation in Chaucer's poetry are a warning not to read the *General Prologue* simply as the work of a medieval sociologist and reporter. There is some likelihood that several of the pilgrims—the Man of Law, the Prioress, the Shipman, the Reeve, and Harry Bailly himself—were based upon individuals whom Chaucer had encountered in the course of his official duties. But the poetic characters formed upon this basis of private experience no longer represented medieval life alone. They had become metaphors through which Chaucer realized the form of his imaginative experience.

The essential character of this experience is indicated by Chaucer's style. What may strike us first about his writing in the *General Prologue* is its forceful directness and immediacy, qualities deriving in part from his habitual use of the verb 'to be' in describing the pilgrims. The simplicity of his statements—'a Monk ther was', 'his heed was balled', 'whit was his berd as is the dayesie' —neither invites nor admits qualification. The thing

exists as Chaucer says, its presence solid and incontro-
vertible. This impression is confirmed by the uncom-
plicated naturalness of Chaucer's images, which are taken
from the most familiar areas of common experience. The
Monk's horse is 'as broun as is a berie', the Friar's eyes
twinkle 'as doon the sterres in the frosty night', the
Franklin's purse is as white as morning milk, and the
threadbare Clerk's mount is 'leene as is a rake'. The
Pardoner has a voice 'as smal as hath a goot', and 'swich
glaringe eyen' as a hare; the Reeve's hair is 'dokked lyk a
preest', and the Miller has a beard as red as a fox. The
adjectives used in describing the pilgrims are usually as
simple and direct. Worthy, gay, bright, fair, fresh, perfect,
sharp, wise, which are among the commonest of Chaucer's
descriptive terms, sometimes derive from their placing the
immediacy and strength that normally we expect only of
metaphor.

> Boold was hir face, and fair, and reed of hewe   (460)

describes the Wife of Bath's appearance in language that
seems to have no literary pretension, yet with a graphic
effect that is almost startling. His matter-of-fact note on
the Shipman's sunburnt face has the same arresting
quality:

> The hoote somer hadde maad his hewe al broun.   (396)

Although he uses an image to suggest the size of the
Miller's huge mouth, the comment derives its force from
the repetition of the commonplace adjective by which
Chaucer suggests its size:

> His mouth as greet was as a greet forneys.   (561)

These three examples of Chaucer's vernacular plainness
of idiom show how little he depends upon formal or

technical devices to make his point. If there is no use of metaphor in the *General Prologue*, its absence is likely to go unnoticed in the density and richness of sensation which the poem throws out. The style of its long opening sentence—courtly in form and language, its more elegant vocabulary and involved development indicating a conscious literary mode—offers a sample of the poetic tradition which Chaucer had abandoned. The comic anticlimax which completes the sentence, as he drops abruptly from the rhapsodic to the prosaic, from the mythological Zephirus to the folk and their rollicking pilgrimage, epitomizes the general change which Chaucer's style had undergone in order to reach this final phase. His description of Emelie in *The Knight's Tale*, or of Criseyde in her 'widewes habit blak',

> Simple of atir and debonaire of chere,
> With ful assured loking and manere

has a delicate charm due in part to its gentler vocabulary and verse-movement; but the impression of character is mild and shadowy where the heroine of *The Miller's Tale* —a highly characteristic figure of Chaucer's late style—is given flavour and bite by a series of natural images:

> Hir mouth was sweete as bragot[1] or the meeth,
> Or hoord of apples leyd in hey or heeth.

Chaucer has exchanged courtly elegance for a greater vitality of expression, adopting as his final idiom the rougher but more richly textured forms and vocabulary of colloquial English. In its racy turn of phrase and pithy commentary, the style of the *General Prologue* is often close to the terse, pungent manner of the proverbial

---

[1] *bragot*, a drink made of honey and ale.

sayings which are scattered plentifully through his work. In the fabliaux, which deal frankly with the ludicrous happenings of everyday life, this style reaches its fullest achievement. The account of the carpenter's preparations for the great flood in *The Miller's Tale* uses language whose coarse-grained, earthy flavour supplements the description by evoking a sense of contact with square-cut timber and rough country food:

> His owene hand he made laddres thre,
> To climben by the ronges and the stalkes
> Unto the tubbes hanginge in the balkes,[1]
> And hem vitailled, bothe trogh and tubbe,
> With breed and chese, and good ale in a jubbe.

These are the colloquial English terms which, after the opening literary flourish of the *General Prologue*, Chaucer accepts as the standard of his narrative. Lifted out of their context, such conversational remarks as

> For aught I woot, he was of Dertemouthe (391)

or, in commenting upon the Clerk,

> And he nas nat right fat, I undertake (290)

read like informal asides taken from everyday speech, with no pretensions to literary character. They may even seem to have no claim to be poetry. By using this direct and richly vernacular style Chaucer is able to secure an effect of sensational reality, in which material objects take on a heightened power, as though seen with the intensity of imaginative insight.

This intensifying of sensation is most obvious in the degree of emphasis which Chaucer brings to his descrip-

[1] *balkes*, beams.

tion of the pilgrims. The absolute finality of the comment which sums up the Monk,

> Now certeinly he was a fair prelaat   (204)

is typical of the emphatic manner by which Chaucer constantly underlines and reinforces his point. His use of simple intensifying adjectives—ful, wel, al—is so characteristic a feature of his style that their repetition may pass unnoticed, even when they appear as frequently as they do in the portrait of the Prioress.[1] The Monk is set down as 'a lord ful fat and in good point', the Man of Law as 'ful riche of excellence', and the epicurean Franklin has 'ful many a fat partrich' waiting to be eaten. The Reeve shaves himself not just closely but 'as ny as ever he kan'. As a ballad-singer the Friar is without rival—'he baar outrely the pris'—and the Host is made impressive by the manly qualities of which 'him lakkede right naught'. Part of the Clerk's outstanding character—his severe economy of speech—is put in a negative form which retains the emphatic force of Chaucer's statements:

> Noght o word spak he moore than was neede.   (306)

The cumulative effect of such insistent comment is most readily seen in the description of the five Gildsmen, who are among the least conspicuous of the pilgrims. Even these figures, whom Chaucer describes collectively, are given a heightened reality by the emphasis that seems to reflect his delighted approval of their costume and bearing:

> Ful fressh and newe hir geere apiked was;
> Hir knives were chaped noght with bras
> But al with silver; wroght ful clene and weel
> Hir girdles and hir pouches everydeel...
> Everich, for the wisdom that he kan,
> Was shaply for to been an alderman.   (367-74)

[1] The word 'ful' is used eleven times.

The strongly affirmative phrases, 'ful fressh and newe', 'ful clene and weel', 'al with silver', and the inclusive terms 'everydeel' and 'everich', as well as the lavish final compliment, are typical of Chaucer's whole-hearted acceptance of the world about him. His enthusiasm is tempered by the critical insight that enables him to comment ironically upon moral character, but his disclosures are impish and without malice. Like his own Host, who offers an expansive welcome to all his guests 'right hertely', but reserves the right to snub and admonish, Chaucer administers rebukes without losing the good-humoured humanity that remains his great attraction. His security of mind is too assured to be disturbed by the moral failings of society, or for him to adopt the destructive outlook of a satirist. His fondness for affirmative and positive terms—ful, wel, al, greet, certeinly—is a stylistic trait by which Chaucer implicitly associates himself with the unlimited abundance and generosity of natural creation. The carpenter who follows Nicholas's suggestion in *The Miller's Tale*,

> And broghte of mighty ale a large quart

provides an emblem of the quality in Chaucer's poetry which made Dryden remark, 'Here is God's plenty'. His tribute is critically just. Both in its great range of human character and temperament, and in its panoramic survey of narrative forms and types, *The Canterbury Tales* displays a creative power to which only nature offers a parallel.

To the natural world in its scenic aspects Chaucer seems almost completely unresponsive. The pilgrimage moves across Kent without reference to the English landscape, and with only occasional mention of towns on or near the route—Deptford, Boughton under Blee and Rochester. The formal description of springtime which opens the *General Prologue* is the only passage of any length dealing with the natural world, and the subject is introduced apparently only for the sake of the comic anti-climax which Chaucer develops. The passage has a deeper significance. Although he is treating a conventional literary theme, Chaucer's description of life beginning to stir and shoot with the returning warmth of April shows the pressure of unusual excitement. The energy of the writing, felt especially in the succession of forceful verbs—perced, bathed, engendred, inspired—and in the bounding vitality of the reference to the 'yonge sonne', make us recognize that Chaucer is describing not the pictorial charm of springtime but its vigorous creative activity. A sense of irresistible movement drives through the passage, from the violent image of the soil being 'perced to the roote' to the complementary picture of the creatures being urged by the great natural purpose of the mating-season;

> So priketh hem nature in hir corages. (11)

The dynamic quality of the verse admits Chaucer's close association with the events which the opening sentence of his poem describes. For him too a great creative impulse is beginning to move. The natural forces which bring warmth and moisture to the earth, encouraging growth and fertility, stand in a direct relationship with the powerful impulse working upon the poet. The release of this generative vitality produces not the flowers and bird-song of an English countryside, but the company of nine-and-twenty who, in their liveliness and individual force of being, remain the enduring proof of Chaucer's richly creative energy.

All great artists, it seems, are consciously aware of the parallel between their own work and the processes which continually renew the life of the natural world. Chaucer was no exception. By putting himself in the *Canterbury Tales* as a shy, ineffectual figure, he makes the pilgrims whom he has brought into existence seem more substantial than himself. They are the living reality, independent of him and impelled by a more purposeful force of being; he the shadow. By their clamorous appetite for experience or single-minded obsession they prove themselves more than the docile puppets of his literary invention; asserting their individuality of character with an energy which strains the Host's authority to its limits. Chaucer pretends to be eclipsed by the physical vitality, the self-assurance or the professional expertise of his pilgrims. But the *General Prologue*, in the positive drive of its verse and its comprehensive grasp of human character, proves how fully the poet possesses the qualities which he assigns to his creatures.

It is his own sense of vital energy which the pilgrims express. The exuberant good health of the Monk, epitomized in the bald head that 'shoon as any glas', is shared by other pilgrims who live and work out of doors: by the Yeoman, whose 'mighty bowe' is an emblem of his muscular strength, and by the Shipman, whose physical toughness has carried him through 'many a tempest'. The Miller, a champion wrestler able to smash down a door with his head, is a still more striking example of robust bodily power. Raw and brutish, and playing a bagpipe as though to make his brawling vulgarity still louder, the Miller is none the less an entirely positive figure, embodying the blind energy of an unharnessed natural force. The Wife of Bath has similar attributes. Her many pilgrimages show her physical resilience, and her five marriages confirm this impression. Her shameless sexuality might condemn her, but the frankness of her bodily appetite reveals a character dominated by the great natural impulse which the opening lines of the *General Prologue* describe. The Squire, a less flamboyant figure, is moved by the same force. His physical strength and agility are combined with a gaiety of spirit—'singinge he was, or floytinge, al the day'—which expresses the carefree assurance of good health. His embroidered gown associates him with springtime, and his lovesick behaviour—

> He sleep namoore than dooth a nightingale (98)

—links him firmly with the tensely excited mood of the mating-season which Chaucer has referred to earlier. The Prioress is described with much more delicate restraint, yet neither her nun's habit nor the poet's respect for her vocation is allowed to conceal the fact of her attractive femininity. The comment, 'hardily, she was not undergrowe', tells us that she had the proper figure of a woman; and at least one physical feature—

> Hir mouth ful smal, and therto softe and reed (153)

—makes us momentarily aware of the warm pulse of her womanly nature. The ambiguous inscription of her brooch confirms this impression; suggesting, beneath the double obscurity of a foreign language and an equivocal use of words, that the Prioress defers to the same instinctive principle as the morally outrageous Wife of Bath.

This unlimited enthusiasm for life is reflected not only in their striking behaviour and dress, but in the possessions which Chaucer attributes to many of the pilgrims. That the vigorous Monk should have 'ful many a deyntee hors' in his stable flouts the rule of poverty to which he is vowed, and his careless prodigality about the money he spends on hunting condemns him still further. Such lavish indulgence seems appropriate to the Monk's unlimited capacity for enjoyment; and Chaucer's comment, 'for no cost wolde he spare', conveys a sense of the Monk's enthusiasm for life as well as of his reckless use of money. The Franklin is open to similar moral censure as a glutton whose dining-table

> Stood redy covered al the longe day   (356)

and whose cook was in trouble if he could not serve a meal at a moment's notice. Yet again, Chaucer's remark, 'Seint Julian he was in his contree', is respectful and complimentary, not ironically disapproving; and when he reaches the hyperbolic climax of his description,

> It snewed in his hous of mete and drinke,   (347)

it becomes impossible to mistake Chaucer's response to such open-handed generosity. The Franklin's house overflows with natural abundance; with incomparable bread and ale, and well-stocked pens and fish-ponds waiting to supply the furiously active cook, who offers his master's guests 'alle deyntees that men koude thinke'. With this background and his private philosophy of living in delight, the Franklin could represent the heaped-up fruitfulness of the natural world at harvest, that withholds nothing in its abundance. His character reveals the same spirit of instinctive and unreckoning generosity, the same pleasure in loading gifts upon those who sit at his table, and the same anger towards whatever obstructs his lavish hospitality. The admission of bad temper in the remark, 'Wo was his cook', seems at first incompatible with the Franklin's genial character, but the force of life which he represents also deals harshly with those who try to frustrate its creative purposes.

The Reeve and the Pardoner are such figures. The opening five lines of the Reeve's portrait insist upon the cold, uncharitable bareness of appearance which serves as warning of his malignant inner nature—the cruelly close-shaven face and docked hair, and the gaunt physique that gives him legs as lean as sticks: 'ther was no calf ysene'. The dwelling-place 'upon an heeth', and his habitual position at the back of the other pilgrims, show the grim unsociability of a man whose energies are devoted to cheating his master and catching out his own subordinates; unrelaxing in his wolf-like watchfulness. 'They were adrad of him as of the deeth', Chaucer remarks; and whether he is referring to plague or to common mortality, the association is imaginatively fitting. The Reeve has neither the inclination nor the power to nourish natural life. Instead, he exerts upon his surroundings an influence that is baleful and arid; checking the human warmth of others by a coldly deliberate malice that derives from a hatred of life itself. Of all the pilgrims, the Reeve alone carries a piece of rusty equipment: a sword whose lack of polish and keen edge symbolizes the unproductive spirit of the man, devitalized by the meanly negative attitude which he has clamped upon himself. Where the Franklin suggests the abundance and generosity of harvest, the

Reeve seems to embody the frozen barrenness of winter, driving life underground by its destructive savagery, and threatening to starve the creative force of nature into submission.

The Clerk, lean and threadbare, and riding an emaciated horse, has some of the Reeve's outward characteristics, but is treated in part as a comic figure. In reducing himself to beggary for the sake of learning, Chaucer seems to suggest, the Clerk is perversely misdirecting his energies without even the satisfaction of achievement:

> For he hadde geten him yet no benefice.   (293)

His physical hollowness supplies an ironic comment on the worth of a pursuit which substitutes book-learning for an immediate personal experience of life. But if the Clerk is mistaken in this choice, he has no hostile feelings towards the creative system from which he has withdrawn. Unlike the Reeve, he does not present a threat to those about him, but rides—in the Host's words—'coy and stille as dooth a maide', immersed in philosophical reflexions. For this reason he can be treated tolerantly where the Reeve's dangerous misanthropy and the Pardoner's fraudulent vitality demand to be mercilessly exposed.

Chaucer the pilgrim makes no pretence of being deceived by the youthful manner which the Pardoner puts on. His love-songs, his careless informality of dress and his fashionable air—'al of the newe jet'—have a plausibility which Chaucer demolishes in a single cutting remark that is final and unanswerable:

> I trowe he were a gelding or a mare.   (693)

The festive spirit or 'jolitee' assumed by the Pardoner is meant to indicate the kind of physical vitality which bubbles over in the Squire, and which gives the Monk his boundless enthusiasm for hunting.[1] But the Squire's gay costume, his light-hearted singing and fluting, are the marks of a genuine high-spirited vigour such as the Pardoner can never possess. 'No berd hadde he,' Chaucer declares flatly, 'ne nevere sholde have.' The Pardoner's imposture of being a virile and attractively wild young man is exposed by his smooth face and lack of beard, and by the lifeless pallor of his hair, falling thinly to his shoulders. His pretence of gaily animated manliness, added to his sexual impotence, arouses Chaucer's biting scorn. Whether in his priestly function or as a man, the Pardoner has nothing to communicate. His religious purpose is a sham as contemptible as the show of masculine temper by which he tries to conceal a humiliating defect. Neither is capable of propagating itself. This lack of creative virtue is reflected in the false relics by which he defrauds his simple congregation, claiming miraculous or restorative powers for a bottle of pig's bones, a trashy metal cross and a scrap of worthless fabric. This collection of rubbish is no more miraculous than the mitten which he offers to the faithful as a means of giving fertility to their crops:

> He that his hand wol putte in this mitayn,
> He shal have multiplying of his grain,
> Whan he hath sowen, be it whete or otes,
> So that he offre pens, or elles grotes.[2]

---

[1] Compare the use of 'jolitee' by the Wife of Bath in the passage quoted on p. 15 above, where the term connotes revelry, finery of dress, and sexual enjoyment.

[2] *grote*, coin worth fourpence.

That the sterile Pardoner should offer such a guarantee of healthy increase is deeply ironic, but the deception has a more serious side. Where the whole appearance of the Reeve declares him a man to be dreaded, the spurious liveliness and 'jolitee' of the Pardoner give colour to his promises of restoring physical and spiritual health. Accepting him as a representative of the natural force which engenders life, his congregation trustfully hands over money in return for services which the Pardoner is incapable of carrying out. By persuading his victims to waste money and hopes upon projects which can never come to fruition, he subverts the process of natural life which he pretends to serve. He is a plausible fake, drawing to himself the reverence due to nature in her creative energy, and charging fees for promising to supply the regenerative power which his own neutered body has been denied.

This is the challenge which the Host meets and throws back at the end of *The Pardoner's Tale*, when the pilgrims are invited to do homage to the emasculated teller and his rubbishy relics. In suggesting that the Host shall begin, the Pardoner attacks the life of the company at its centre. Not only is Harry Bailly its acknowledged leader, whose example the other pilgrims will sheepishly follow if he gives way. In the self-assured manliness of which he 'lakkede right naught' he is also the outstanding figure of the vital force which the Pardoner is trying to supplant by an impotent sham. Their clash represents a direct confrontation of robust creative life by a sterile dummy seeking to usurp its functions and authority. The Host's reaction to the challenge is immediate and explosive. His point-blank reference to the Pardoner's lack of reproductive organs—'Lat kutte hem of, I wol thee helpe hem carie'—completes his scornful repudiation of the man's false credentials, and destroys the Pardoner's bid for moral leadership by exposing him to ridicule. The repulse is annihilating:

> This Pardoner answerde nat a word;
> So wrooth he was, no word ne wolde he seye.

His speechlessness shows that the moment of danger has passed. Life has proved too vigorous and creatively positive to be checked more than momentarily by the Pardoner's claim to respect, as a man embodying—and offering for sale—its own generative power.

The episode typifies the optimistic spirit of *The Canterbury Tales*. It shows that Chaucer is not disposed to celebrate, simply and uncritically, the creative triumph which his poem both describes and represents in its own imaginative terms. While he recognizes the driving energy of the natural world and associates himself with it, he acknowledges too that its vitality and abundance are threatened by negative forces, whose purpose is to bring to a standstill the system which nourishes and renews natural life. The presence of the Pardoner, the Reeve and the revoltingly disfigured Summoner among the company of exuberantly healthy pilgrims admits the threat of diseased and parasitic forms of life, stunting development and sapping the vigour of growing things. The overthrow of the sexually lifeless Pardoner by the Host is a defeat as symbolic as the repulse of the winter-spirit by the blazing energy of the god of summer, or as the breaking of frost and drought by warm showers and sunshine, which the first sentence of the *General Prologue* describes. Life may suffer set-backs, but not be permanently checked or damaged.

The triumph of its greater vitality has a particular significance within Chaucer's poem. His own activity as poet, the *General Prologue* implies, has its own period of re-awakening as a surge of imaginative energy brings him a new access of creative power. Some such forward bound gave him the simple, inspired conception of uniting tales and tellers—the representative types of literature and of humanity—in the last and greatest of his works. The confident power and authority which he attributes to the pilgrims, we have seen, are his own: his too the inexhaustible force of life by which, like nature, he brings into existence a succession of fresh and astonishing beings. If, in the Pardoner, there is some hint of a conflict within himself which checks this exhilarating process, it is swept away by the commanding sanity and self-assurance of the Host: a figure who, from the moment when he 'gadrede us togidre alle in a flok', never loses paternal control of his creatures and their wayward moods. Not even his vituperative assault upon the Pardoner disturbs the community of the group, or the progress of the competition, for long. The Knight makes one of his few descents into the arena to reconcile the quarrel, proposing amicably that they continue their interrupted game: 'as we diden, lat us laughe and pleye'. The sequel, immediately typical of Chaucer, sends the pilgrims forward again as a body at one with itself, assured of its purpose and wrapped in a final content of spirit:

Anon they kiste, and riden forth hir weye.

THE ARRANGEMENT OF THE
CANTERBURY TALES

As the Introduction points out, *The Canterbury Tales* is an unfinished work. Excluding the Host, who as arbiter would not be expected to contribute a tale, there are thirty-two pilgrims in the company. Of this number, only twenty-three are called forward to tell stories, and only Chaucer himself relates more than one tale. As several of the linking passages are missing, these twenty-four stories do not form a continuous narrative chain but ten separate fragments, varying in length from a single prologue and tale to a linked series of six tales. The order of these fragments in the Chaucer manuscripts does not coincide with stages in the progress of the pilgrimage: in fact, some of the tales told near Canterbury are given places in the earlier groups of stories. An alternative sequence has been suggested, but as Chaucer evidently did not leave the fragments in any finally determined order, their arrangement in the manuscripts is as logical as any other. It runs as shown below. Asterisks denote the tales which have no separate introduction or prologue.

Fragment I: *The General Prologue*
                        The Knight's Tale
                        The Miller's Tale
                        The Reeve's Tale
                        The Cook's Tale (unfinished)

Fragment II: *The Man of Law's Tale*

Fragment III: *The Wife of Bath's Tale*
                        The Friar's Tale
                        The Summoner's Tale

Arrangement of 'The Canterbury Tales'

Fragment IV: *The Clerk's Tale*
                      The Merchant's Tale

Fragment V: *The Squire's Tale* (interrupted)
                      The Franklin's Tale

Fragment VI: *The Physician's Tale★*
                      The Pardoner's Tale

Fragment VII: *The Shipman's Tale★*
                      The Prioress's Tale
                      Chaucer's Tale of Sir Thopas (interrupted)
                      Chaucer's Tale of Melibee
                      The Monk's Tale (interrupted)
                      The Nun's Priest's Tale

Fragment VIII: *The Second Nun's Tale*
                      The Canon's Yeoman's Tale

Fragment IX: *The Manciple's Tale*

Fragment X: *The Parson's Tale*

CHAUCER'S ENGLISH

Chaucer wrote in Middle English, a form of the language current between about 1150 and 1500. Its grammar and vocabulary reflect the influence of other languages, predominantly Anglo-Saxon, French and German. For this reason Middle English is not immediately familiar to the modern reader. The notes to this edition of the *General Prologue* translate difficult phrases, and the glossary gives modern equivalents for single words which have either changed their form or dropped out of use. Chaucer's verse-form and scansion are discussed in the introductory volume to this series. The following notes, intended as hints to the beginner, list only words and grammatical forms found in the *General Prologue*.

VERBS

Infinitives end in *-n*; as in *to goon*, to go or to walk; *to seken*, to seek; *to ben*, to be; and *to stonden*, to stand. *Stonden* shows the very frequent substitution of *o* for the modern *a* (see below).

Past participles often begin with *y-*: as in *yronne*, run; *yfalle*, fallen; *yknowe*, disclosed; and *ytaught*, informed. *Yclepen*, called, from the infinitive *clepen*, is an example of participle form closer to modern English.

Plural forms sometimes appear in *-n*: as in *they weren*, they were; and *that slepen*, that sleep.

The negative is usually formed by prefixing *ne* to the verb; as in *ne was*, was not; *he ne knew*, he did not know; and *n'arette*, do not impute. In the case of common verbs the prefix is often absorbed into the word, as in *nas=ne was*, was not, and *noot* = *ne woot*, did not know. Double negatives are plentifully used: *nas nat*, was not; *ne lefte nat*, did not leave; *nowher noon*, nowhere any; *nas noon swich*, was no such.

'KAN' AND 'KNOWEN'

In modern English the same verb is used to denote two distinct kinds of knowing; those represented in French by *savoir* and *connaître*, and in German by *können* and *wissen*. Middle English allowed the same distinction to be made between practical ability, or know-how, and intellectual grasp. *Kan* and *koude* convey the sense of knowing how to do something, or of possessing special talent or expertise. The modern forms 'can' and 'could' are not a satisfactory equivalent for these strong Middle English verbs. Thus:

wel koude he sitte on hors = he was an expert horseman.

noon that kan so muchel of daliaunce = no one who knows so well how to be charming and amusing.

she koude of that art the olde daunce = she knew all the ins and outs of that game.

Knowen is used to describe various kinds of intellectual activity—distinguishing, recognising, detecting, understanding, and so on. This verb cannot usually be translated simply as 'to know'. Thus,

he knew the tavernes wel = he was well acquainted with the taverns.

that he ne knew his sleighte = but he detected his cheating.

and knew hir conseil = and made himself familiar with their secrets.

The distinction of sense between *kan* and *knowen* is illustrated by Chaucer's comment on the Cook,

wel koude he knowe a draughte of Londoun ale = he was an expert taster of London ale.

46

SPELLING

Among old spellings the commonest forms are:

In pronouns, *h* for the modern *th*; as in *hem* for them, and *hir* or *hire* for their. But note that *hir* is also used for her.

Initial *y* in place of the modern *g*; as in *yeve*, *yaf*, for give, gave, and *yeldehalle* for gildhall. Used internally, the substituted *y* produces *foryete*, forget, and *foryeven*, forgiven.

Terminal *-we* in nouns now ending *-ow*; as in *arwe* for arrow, *halwes* for hallows, *morwe* for morrow and *pilwe* for pillow; and in adjectives, *holwe* for hollow. Similarly, terminal *-ne* where the modern form is *-en*, as in *festne* for fasten, *chiknes* for chickens.

As noted above, internal *o* frequently occurs where *a* now appears; as in *lond* for land, *stonde* for stand, *strondes* for strands = shores. Compare *dronken* for drunken, *song* for sung, and *dong* for dung.

Double vowels give an unfamiliar appearance to words which have now either dropped one or adopted a terminal *e* in place of the doubled letter: thus *caas* for case, *estaat* for estate, *maad* for made and *smoot* for smote; and *reed* for red, *leet* for let, *boold* for bold.

SOME DECEPTIVE PHRASES

hem thoughte = it seemed to them (*hem* is dative; compare *as it thoughte me*).

him was levere = he would rather (literally, it was preferable to him).

which they weren = who, or what kind of people, they were.

In several adverbial phrases, 'that' is intrusive, e.g. *whan that* = when, *er that* = before, *al be that* = although, *how that* = how, *sin that* = since.

Some of the terms derived immediately from French are deceptive in meaning, e.g. *aventure* does not mean adventure but chance. *Verray* = true, truly; *pleyn* = full, fully, and *port* = demeanour. Note too that *fredom* does not mean freedom but generosity.

NOTE ON THE TEXT

The text which follows is based upon that of F. N. Robinson (*The Complete Works of Geoffrey Chaucer*, 2nd ed., 1957).[1] The punctuation has been revised, with special reference to the exclamation marks. Spelling has been partly rationalized, by substituting *i* for *y* wherever the change does not affect the semantic value of the word. Thus *smylyng* becomes 'smiling', and *nyghtyngale* 'nightingale', but *wyn* (wine), *lyk* (like), and *fyr* (fire) are allowed to stand.

No accentuation has been provided in this text, for two reasons. First, because it produces a page displeasing to the eye; secondly, because it no longer seems necessary or entirely reliable in the light of modern scholarship. It is not now thought that the later works of Chaucer were written in a ten-syllable line from which no variation was permissible. The correct reading of a line of Chaucer is now seen to be more closely related to the correct reading of a comparable line of prose with phrasing suited to the rhythms of speech. This allows the reader to be more flexible in his interpretation of the line, and makes it unreasonably pedantic to provide a rigid system of accentuation.

NOTE ON PRONUNCIATION

These equivalences are intended to offer only a rough guide. For further detail, see the Introductory Volume to this series.

SHORT VOWELS

ă represents the sound now written *u*, as in 'cut'
ĕ as in modern 'set'
ĭ as in modern 'is'
ŏ as in modern 'top'
ŭ as in modern 'put' (not as in 'cut')
final -*e* represents the neutral vowel sound in '*a*bout' or 'atten*tio*n'. It is silent when the next word in the line begins with a vowel or an *h*.

---

[1] Two lines acknowledged as authentic by Robinson have been incorporated into the text following line 253. For this reason, line-references after this point of the present edition do not correspond with those of some other editions of the *General Prologue*.

Note on the Text

LONG VOWELS

ā as in modern 'car' (not as in 'name')

ē (open—i.e. where the equivalent modern word is spelt with *ea*) as in modern 'there'

ē (close—i.e. where the equivalent modern word is spelt with *ee* or *e*) represents the sound now written *a* as in 'take'

ī as in modern 'machine' (not as in 'like')

ō (open—i.e. where the equivalent modern vowel is pronounced as in 'br*o*ther', 'm*oo*d', or 'g*oo*d') represents the sound now written *aw* as in 'fawn'

ō (close—i.e. where the equivalent modern vowel is pronounced as in 'road') as in modern 'note'

ū as in French *tu* or German *Tür*

DIPHTHONGS

ai and *ei* both roughly represent the sound now written *i* or *y* as in 'die' or 'dye'

au and *aw* both represent the sound now written *ow* or *ou* as in 'now' or 'pounce'

ou and *ow* have two pronunciations: as in *through* where the equivalent modern vowel is pronounced as in 'through' or 'mouse'; and as in *pounce* where the equivalent modern vowel is pronounced as in 'know' or 'thought'

WRITING OF VOWELS AND DIPHTHONGS

A long vowel is often indicated by doubling, as in *roote* or *eek*. The *ŭ* sound is sometimes represented by an *o* as in *yong*. The *au* sound is sometimes represented by an *a*, especially before *m* or *n*, as in *cha(u)mbre* or *cha(u)nce*.

CONSONANTS

Largely as in modern English, except that many consonants now silent were still pronounced. *Gh* was pronounced as in Scottish 'lo*ch*', and both consonants should be pronounced in such groups as the following: '*gn*acchen', '*kn*ave', '*w*or*d*', 'fo*lk*', '*wr*ong'.

THE GENERAL PROLOGUE

Here biginneth the Book of the Tales of Caunterbury

Whan that Aprill with his shoures soote
The droghte of March hath perced to the roote,
And bathed every veine in swich licour
Of which vertu engendred is the flour;
Whan Zephirus eek with his sweete breeth
Inspired hath in every holt and heeth
The tendre croppes, and the yonge sonne
Hath in the Ram his halve cours yronne,
And smale foweles maken melodie,
That slepen al the night with open ye   10
(So priketh hem nature in hir corages);
Thanne longen folk to goon on pilgrimages,
And palmeres for to seken straunge strondes,
To ferne halwes, kowthe in sondry londes;
And specially from every shires ende
Of Engelond to Caunterbury they wende,
The hooly blisful martir for to seke,
That hem hath holpen whan that they were seeke.
   Bifil that in that seson on a day,
In Southwerk at the Tabard as I lay   20
Redy to wenden on my pilgrimage
To Caunterbury with ful devout corage,
At night was come into that hostelrie
Wel nine and twenty in a compaignie,
Of sondry folk, by aventure yfalle
In felaweshipe, and pilgrimes were they alle,
That toward Caunterbury wolden ride.

The chambres and the stables weren wide,

And wel we weren esed atte beste.

30 And shortly, whan the sonne was to reste,

So hadde I spoken with hem everichon

That I was of hir felaweshipe anon,

And made forward erly for to rise,

To take oure wey ther as I yow devise.

But nathelees, whil I have time and space,

Er that I ferther in this tale pace,

Me thinketh it acordaunt to resoun

To telle yow al the condicioun

Of ech of hem, so as it semed me,

40 And whiche they weren, and of what degree,

And eek in what array that they were inne;

And at a knight than wol I first biginne.

A KNIGHT ther was, and that a worthy man,

That fro the time that he first bigan

To riden out, he loved chivalrie,

Trouthe and honour, fredom and curteisie.

Ful worthy was he in his lordes werre,

And therto hadde he riden, no man ferre,

As wel in cristendom as in hethenesse,

50 And evere honoured for his worthinesse.

At Alisaundre he was whan it was wonne.

Ful ofte time he hadde the bord bigonne

Aboven alle nacions in Pruce;

In Lettow hadde he reysed and in Ruce,

No Cristen man so ofte of his degree.

In Gernade at the seege eek hadde he be

Of Algezir, and riden in Belmarie.

At Lyeys was he and at Satalie,

Whan they were wonne; and in the Grete See

52

At many a noble armee hadde he be.   60
At mortal batailles hadde he been fiftene,
And foughten for oure feith at Tramissene
In listes thries, and ay slain his foo.
This ilke worthy knight hadde been also
Sometime with the Lord of Palatie
Again another hethen in Turkie.
And everemoore he hadde a sovereyn prys;
And though that he were worthy, he was wys,
And of his port as meeke as is a maide.
He nevere yet no vileynie ne saide   70
In al his lif unto no maner wight.
He was a verray, parfit gentil knight.
But, for to tellen yow of his array,
His hors were goode, but he was nat gay.
Of fustian he wered a gipon
Al bismotered with his habergeon,
For he was late ycome from his viage,
And wente for to doon his pilgrimage.

  With him ther was his sone, a yong SQUIER,
A lovyere and a lusty bacheler,   80
With lokkes crulle as they were leyd in presse.
Of twenty yeer of age he was, I gesse.
Of his stature he was of evene lengthe,
And wonderly delivere, and of greet strengthe.
And he hadde been somtime in chivachie
In Flaundres, in Artois, and Picardie,
And born him weel, as of so litel space,
In hope to stonden in his lady grace.
Embrouded was he, as it were a meede
Al ful of fresshe floures, white and reede.   90
Singinge he was, or floytinge, al the day;

53

He was as fressh as is the month of May.
Short was his gowne, with sleves longe and wide.
Wel koude he sitte on hors and faire ride.
He koude songes make and wel endite,
Juste and eek daunce, and weel purtreye and write.
So hoote he lovede that by nightertale
He sleep namoore than dooth a nightingale.
Curteis he was, lowely, and servisable,
And carf biforn his fader at the table.

A YEMAN hadde he and servantz namo
At that time, for him liste ride so,
And he was clad in cote and hood of grene.
A sheef of pecok arwes, bright and kene,
Under his belt he bar ful thriftily,
(Wel koude he dresse his takel yemanly:
His arwes drouped noght with fetheres lowe)
And in his hand he baar a mighty bowe.
A not heed hadde he, with a broun visage.
Of wodecraft wel koude he al the usage.
Upon his arm he baar a gay bracer,
And by his side a swerd and a bokeler,
And on that oother side a gay daggere
Harneised wel and sharp as point of spere;
A Cristopher on his brest of silver sheene.
An horn he bar, the bawdrik was of grene;
A forster was he, soothly, as I gesse.

Ther was also a Nonne, a PRIORESSE,
That of hir smiling was ful simple and coy;
Hire gretteste ooth was but by Seinte Loy;
And she was cleped madame Eglentine.
Ful weel she soong the service divine,
Entuned in hir nose ful semely,

100

110

120

54

And Frenssh she spak ful faire and fetisly,
After the scole of Stratford atte Bowe,
For Frenssh of Paris was to hire unknowe.
At mete wel ytaught was she with alle:
She leet no morsel from hir lippes falle,
Ne wette hir fingres in hir sauce depe;
Wel koude she carie a morsel and wel kepe   130
That no drope ne fille upon hire brest.
In curteisie was set ful muchel hir lest.
Hir over-lippe wiped she so clene
That in hir coppe ther was no ferthing sene
Of grece, whan she dronken hadde hir draughte.
Ful semely after hir mete she raughte.
And sikerly she was of greet desport,
And ful plesaunt, and amiable of port,
And peyned hire to countrefete cheere
Of court, and to been estatlich of manere,   140
And to ben holden digne of reverence.
But, for to speken of hire conscience,
She was so charitable and so pitous
She wolde wepe, if that she saugh a mous
Kaught in a trappe, if it were deed or bledde.
Of smale houndes hadde she that she fedde
With rosted flessh, or milk and wastel-breed.
But soore wepte she if oon of hem were deed,
Or if men smoot it with a yerde smerte;
And al was conscience and tendre herte.   150
Ful semely hir wimpul pinched was,
Hir nose tretis, hir eyen greye as glas,
Hir mouth ful smal, and therto softe and reed;
But sikerly she hadde a fair forheed;
It was almoost a spanne brood, I trowe;

For, hardily, she was nat undergrowe.
Ful fetis was hir cloke, as I was war.
Of smal coral aboute hire arm she bar
A peire of bedes, gauded al with grene,
And theron heng a brooch of gold ful sheene,
On which ther was first write a crowned A,
And after *Amor vincit omnia.*

Another NONNE with hire hadde she,
That was hir chapeleyne, and preestes thre.

A MONK ther was, a fair for the maistrie,
An outridere, that lovede venerie,
A manly man, to been an abbot able.
Ful many a deyntee hors hadde he in stable,
And whan he rood, men mighte his bridel heere
Ginglen in a whistlinge wind als cleere
And eek as loude as dooth the chapel belle
Ther as this lord was kepere of the celle.
The reule of Seint Maure or of Seint Beneit,
By cause that it was old and somdel streit
This ilke Monk leet olde thinges pace,
And heeld after the newe world the space.
He yaf nat of that text a pulled hen,
That seith that hunters ben nat hooly men,
Ne that a monk, whan he is recchelees,
Is likned til a fissh that is waterlees,—
This is to seyn, a monk out of his cloistre.
But thilke text heeld he nat worth an oystre;
And I seyde his opinion was good.
What sholde he studie and make himselven wood,
Upon a book in cloistre alwey to poure,
Or swinken with his handes, and laboure,
As Austin bit? How shal the world be served?

Lat Austin have his swink to him reserved!
Therfore he was a prikasour aright:
Grehoundes he hadde as swift as fowel in flight;   190
Of priking and of hunting for the hare
Was al his lust, for no cost wolde he spare.
I seigh his sleves purfiled at the hond
With gris, and that the fineste of a lond;
And, for to festne his hood under his chin,
He hadde of gold ywroght a ful curious pin;
A love-knotte in the gretter ende ther was.
His heed was balled, that shoon as any glas,
And eek his face, as he hadde been enoint.
He was a lord ful fat and in good point;   200
His eyen stepe, and rollinge in his heed,
That stemed as a forneys of a leed;
His bootes souple, his hors in greet estaat.
Now certeinly he was a fair prelaat;
He was nat pale as a forpined goost.
A fat swan loved he best of any roost.
His palfrey was as broun as is a berie.
   A FRERE ther was, a wantowne and a merie,
A limitour, a ful solempne man.
In alle the ordres foure is noon that kan   210
So muchel of daliaunce and fair langage.
He hadde maad ful many a mariage
Of yonge wommen at his owene cost.
Unto his ordre he was a noble post.
Ful wel biloved and famulier was he
With frankeleyns over al in his contree,
And eek with worthy wommen of the toun;
For he hadde power of confessioun,
As seyde himself, moore than a curat,

220 For of his ordre he was licenciat.
Ful swetely herde he confessioun,
And plesaunt was his absolucioun:
He was an esy man to yeve penaunce,
Ther as he wiste to have a good pitaunce.
For unto a povre ordre for to yive
Is signe that a man is wel yshrive;
For if he yaf, he dorste make avaunt,
He wiste that a man was repentaunt;
For many a man so hard is of his herte,
230 He may nat wepe, althogh him soore smerte.
Therfore in stede of wepinge and preyeres
Men moote yeve silver to the povre freres.
His tipet was ay farsed ful of knives
And pinnes, for to yeven faire wives.
And certeinly he hadde a murie note:
Wel koude he singe and pleyen on a rote;
Of yeddinges he baar outrely the prys.
His nekke whit was as the flour-de-lys;
Therto he strong was as a champioun.
240 He knew the tavernes wel in every toun
And everich hostiler and tappestere
Bet than a lazar or a beggestere;
For unto swich a worthy man as he
Acorded nat, as by his facultee,
To have with sike lazars aqueyntaunce.
It is nat honest, it may nat avaunce,
For to deelen with no swich poraille,
But al with riche and selleres of vitaille.
And over al, ther as profit sholde arise,
250 Curteis he was and lowely of servise.
Ther nas no man nowher so vertuous.

He was the beste beggere in his hous;
And yaf a certeyn ferme for the graunt;
Noon of his bretheren cam ther in his haunt;
For thogh a widwe hadde noght a sho,
So plesaunt was his ' *In principio*,'
Yet wolde he have a ferthing, er he wente.
His purchas was wel bettre than his rente.
And rage he koude, as it were right a whelp.
In love-dayes ther koude he muchel help,   260
For ther he was nat lik a cloisterer
With a thredbare cope, as is a povre scoler,
But he was lyk a maister or a pope.
Of double worstede was his semicope,
That rounded as a belle out of the presse.
Somwhat he lipsed, for his wantownesse,
To make his Englissh sweete upon his tonge;
And in his harping, whan that he hadde songe,
His eyen twinkled in his heed aright,
As doon the sterres in the frosty night.   270
This worthy limitour was cleped Huberd.

A MARCHANT was ther with a forked berd,
In mottelee, and hye on horse he sat;
Upon his heed a Flaundrissh bever hat,
His bootes clasped faire and fetisly.
His resons he spak ful solempnely,
Sowninge alwey th'encrees of his winning.
He wolde the see were kept for any thing
Bitwixe Middelburgh and Orewelle.
Wel koude he in eschaunge sheeldes selle.   280
This worthy man ful wel his wit bisette:
Ther wiste no wight that he was in dette,
So estatly was he of his governaunce

With his bargaines and with his chevissaunce.
For sothe he was a worthy man with alle,
But, sooth to seyn, I noot how men him calle.
    A CLERK ther was of Oxenford also,
That unto logik hadde longe ygo.
As leene was his hors as is a rake,
290   And he nas nat right fat, I undertake,
But looked holwe, and therto sobrely.
Ful thredbare was his overeste courtepy;
For he hadde geten him yet no benefice,
Ne was so worldly for to have office.
For him was levere have at his beddes heed
Twenty bookes, clad in blak or reed,
Of Aristotle and his philosophie,
Than robes riche, or fithele, or gay sautrie.
But al be that he was a philosophre,
300   Yet hadde he but litel gold in cofre;
But al that he mighte of his freendes hente,
On bookes and on lerninge he it spente,
And bisily gan for the soules preye
Of hem that yaf him wherwith to scoleye.
Of studie took he moost cure and moost heede.
Noght o word spak he moore than was neede,
And that was seyd in forme and reverence,
And short and quik and ful of hy sentence;
Sowninge in moral vertu was his speche,
310   And gladly wolde he lerne and gladly teche.
    A SERGEANT OF THE LAWE, war and wys,
That often hadde been at the Parvis,
Ther was also, ful riche of excellence.
Discreet he was and of greet reverence—
He semed swich, his wordes weren so wise.

Justice he was ful often in assise,
By patente and by pleyn commissioun.
For his science and for his heigh renoun,
Of fees and robes hadde he many oon.
So greet a purchasour was nowher noon: 320
Al was fee simple to him in effect;
His purchasing mighte nat been infect.
Nowher so bisy a man as he ther nas,
And yet he semed bisier than he was.
In termes hadde he caas and doomes alle
That from the time of king William were falle.
Therto he koude endite, and make a thing,
Ther koude no wight pinche at his writing;
And every statut koude he pleyn by rote
He rood but hoomly in a medlee cote,   330
Girt with a ceint of silk, with barres smale;
Of his array telle I no lenger tale.

   A FRANKELEYN was in his compaignie.
Whit was his berd as is the dayesie;
Of his complexioun he was sangwin.
Wel loved he by the morwe a sop in wyn;
To liven in delit was evere his wone,
For he was Epicurus owene sone,
That heeld opinioun that pleyn delit
Was verray felicitee parfit.   340
An housholdere, and that a greet, was he;
Seint Julian he was in his contree.
His breed, his ale, was alweys after oon;
A bettre envined man was nowher noon.
Withoute bake mete was nevere his hous
Of fissh and flessh, and that so plentevous,
It snewed in his hous of mete and drinke,

Of alle deyntees that men koude thinke.
After the sondry sesons of the yeer,
350 So chaunged he his mete and his soper.
Ful many a fat partrich hadde he in muwe,
And many a breem and many a luce in stuwe.
Wo was his cook but if his sauce were
Poynaunt and sharp, and redy al his geere.
His table dormant in his halle alway
Stood redy covered al the longe day.
At sessiouns ther was he lord and sire;
Ful ofte time he was knight of the shire.
An anlaas and a gipser al of silk
360 Heeng at his girdel, whit as morne milk.
A shirreve hadde he been, and a contour.
Was nowher swich a worthy vavasour.

AN HABERDASSHERE and a CARPENTER,
A WEBBE, a DYERE, and a TAPICER,—
And they were clothed alle in o liveree
Of a solempne and a greet fraternitee.
Ful fressh and newe hir geere apiked was;
Hir knives were chaped noght with bras
But al with silver; wroght ful clene and weel
370 Hire girdles and hir pouches everydeel.
Wel semed ech of hem a fair burgeys
To sitten in a yeldehalle on a deis.
Everich, for the wisdom that he kan,
Was shaply for to been an alderman.
For catel hadde they ynogh and rente,
And eek hir wives wolde it wel assente;
And elles certeyn were they to blame.
It is ful fair to been ycleped 'madame,'
And goon to vigilies al bifore,

And have a mantel roialliche ybore. 380
   A COOK they hadde with hem for the nones
To boille the chiknes with the marybones,
And poudre-marchant tart and galingale.
Wel koude he knowe a draughte of Londoun ale.
He koude rooste, and sethe, and broille, and frie,
Maken mortreux, and wel bake a pie.
But greet harm was it, as it thoughte me,
That on his shine a mormal hadde he.
For blankmanger, that made he with the beste.

   A SHIPMAN was ther, woninge fer by weste; 390
For aught I woot, he was of Dertemouthe.
He rood upon a rouncy, as he kouthe,
In a gowne of falding to the knee.
A daggere hanginge on a laas hadde he
Aboute his nekke, under his arm adoun.
The hoote somer hadde maad his hewe al broun;
And certeinly he was a good felawe.
Ful many a draughte of wyn had he ydrawe
Fro Burdeux-ward, whil that the chapman sleep.
Of nice conscience took he no keep. 400
If that he faught, and hadde the hyer hond,
By water he sente hem hoom to every lond.
But of his craft to rekene wel his tides,
His stremes, and his daungers him bisides,
His herberwe, and his moone, his lodemenage,
Ther nas noon swich from Hulle to Cartage.
Hardy he was and wys to undertake;
With many a tempest hadde his berd been shake.
He knew alle the havenes, as they were,
Fro Gootlond to the cape of Finistere, 410
And every crike in Britaigne and in Spaine.

His barge ycleped was the Maudelaine.

    With us ther was a DOCTOUR OF PHISIK;
In al this world ne was ther noon him lik,
To speke of phisik and of surgerye,
For he was grounded in astronomye.
He kepte his pacient a ful greet deel
In houres by his magik natureel.
Wel koude he fortunen the ascendent
420   Of his images for his pacient.
He knew the cause of everich maladie,
Were it of hoot, or coold, or moist, or drie,
And where they engendred, and of what humour.
He was a verray, parfit praktisour:
The cause yknowe, and of his harm the roote,
Anon he yaf the sike man his boote.
Ful redy hadde he his apothecaries
To sende him drogges and his letuaries,
For ech of hem made oother for to winne—
430   Hir frendshipe nas nat newe to biginne.
Wel knew he the olde Esculapius,
And Deiscorides, and eek Rufus,
Olde Ypocras, Hali, and Galien,
Serapion, Razis, and Avicen,
Averrois, Damascien, and Constantin,
Bernard, and Gatesden, and Gilbertin.
Of his diete mesurable was he,
For it was of no superfluitee,
But of greet norissing and digestible.
440   His studie was but litel on the Bible.
In sangwin and in pers he clad was al,
Lined with taffata and with sendal;
And yet he was but esy of dispence;

He kepte that he wan in pestilence.
For gold in phisik is a cordial,
Therefore he lovede gold in special.
   A good WIF was ther OF biside BATHE,
But she was somdel deef, and that was scathe.
Of clooth-making she hadde swich an haunt,
She passed hem of Ypres and of Gaunt.   450
In al the parisshe wif ne was ther noon
That to the offringe bifore hire sholde goon;
And if ther dide, certeyn so wrooth was she,
That she was out of alle charitee.
Hir coverchiefs ful fine weren of ground;
I dorste swere they weyeden ten pound
That on a Sonday weren upon hir heed.
Hir hosen weren of fyn scarlet reed,
Ful streite yteyd, and shoes ful moiste and
     newe.
Boold was hir face, and fair, and reed of hewe.   460
She was a worthy womman al hir live:
Housbondes at chirche dore she hadde five,
Withouten oother compaignye in youthe,—
But therof nedeth nat to speke as nowthe.
And thries hadde she been at Jerusalem;
She hadde passed many a straunge strem;
At Rome she hadde been, and at Boloigne,
In Galice at Seint-Jame, and at Coloigne.
She koude muchel of wandringe by the weye.
Gat-tothed was she, soothly for to seye.   470
Upon an amblere esily she sat,
Ywimpled wel, and on hir heed an hat
As brood as is a bokeler or a targe;
A foot-mantel aboute hir hipes large,

And on hir feet a paire of spores sharpe.
In felaweshipe wel koude she laughe and carpe.
Of remedies of love she knew per chaunce,
For she koude of that art the olde daunce.
    A good man was ther of religioun,
480   And was a povre PERSOUN OF A TOUN,
But riche he was of hooly thoght and werk.
He was also a lerned man, a clerk,
That Cristes gospel trewely wolde preche;
His parisshens devoutly wolde he teche.
Benigne he was, and wonder diligent,
And in adversitee ful pacient,
And swich he was ypreved ofte sithes.
Ful looth were him to cursen for his tithes,
But rather wolde he yeven, out of doute,
490   Unto his povre parisshens aboute
Of his offring and eek of his substaunce.
He koude in litel thing have suffisaunce.
Wyd was his parisshe, and houses fer asonder,
But he ne lefte nat, for reyn ne thonder,
In siknesse nor in meschief to visite
The ferreste in his parisshe, muche and lite,
Upon his feet, and in his hand a staf.
This noble ensample to his sheep he yaf,
That first he wroghte, and afterward he taughte.
500   Out of the gospel he tho wordes caughte,
And this figure he added eek therto,
That if gold ruste, what shal iren do?
For if a preest be foul, on whom we truste,
No wonder is a lewed man to ruste;
And shame it is, if a prest take keep,
A shiten shepherde and a clene sheep.

Wel oghte a preest ensample for to yive,
By his clennesse, how that his sheep sholde
 live.
He sette nat his benefice to hire
And leet his sheep encombred in the mire   510
And ran to Londoun unto Seinte Poules
To seken him a chaunterie for soules,
Or with a bretherhed to been withholde;
But dwelte at hoom, and kepte wel his folde,
So that the wolf ne made it nat miscarie;
He was a shepherde and noght a mercenarie.
And though he hooly were and vertuous,
He was to sinful men nat despitous,
Ne of his speche daungerous ne digne,
But in his teching discreet and benigne.   520
To drawen folk to hevene by fairnesse,
By good ensample, this was his bisynesse.
But it were any persone obstinat,
What so he were, of heigh or lough estat,
Him wolde he snibben sharply for the nonis.
A bettre preest I trowe that nowher noon is.
He waited after no pompe and reverence,
Ne maked him a spiced conscience,
But Cristes loore and his apostles twelve
He taughte, but first he folwed it himselve.   530
   With him ther was a PLOWMAN, was his brother,
That hadde ylad of dong ful many a fother;
A trewe swinkere and a good was he,
Livinge in pees and parfit charitee.
God loved he best with al his hoole herte
At alle times, thogh him gamed or smerte,
And thanne his neighebor right as himselve.

He wolde thresshe, and therto dike and delve,
For Cristes sake, for every povre wight,
540 Withouten hire, if it lay in his might.
His tithes paide he ful faire and wel,
Bothe of his propre swink and his catel.
In a tabard he rood upon a mere.

Ther was also a REVE, and a MILLERE,
A SOMNOUR, and a PARDONER also,
A MAUNCIPLE, and myself—ther were namo.

The MILLERE was a stout carl for the nones;
Ful big he was of brawn, and eek of bones.
That proved wel, for over al ther he cam,
550 At wrastlinge he wolde have alwey the ram.
He was short-sholdred, brood, a thikke knarre;
Ther was no dore that he nolde heve of harre,
Or breke it at a renning with his heed.
His berd as any sowe or fox was reed,
And therto brood, as though it were a spade.
Upon the cop right of his nose he hade
A werte, and theron stood a toft of heris,
Reed as the brustles of a sowes eris;
His nosethirles blake were and wide.
560 A swerd and bokeler bar he by his side.
His mouth as greet was as a greet forneys.
He was a janglere and a goliardeys,
And that was moost of sinne and harlotries.
Wel koude he stelen corn and tollen thries;
And yet he hadde a thombe of gold, pardee.
A whit cote and a blew hood wered he.
A baggepipe wel koude he blowe and sowne,
And therwithal he broghte us out of towne.

A gentil MAUNCIPLE was ther of a temple,

Of which achatours mighte take exemple 570
For to be wise in byinge of vitaille;
For wheither that he paide or took by taille,
Algate he waited so in his achaat
That he was ay biforn and in good staat.
Now is nat that of God a ful fair grace
That swich a lewed mannes wit shal pace
The wisdom of an heep of lerned men?
Of maistres hadde he mo than thries ten,
That weren of lawe expert and curious,
Of which ther were a duszeyne in that hous 580
Worthy to been stiwardes of rente and lond
Of any lord that is in Engelond,
To make him live by his propre good
In honour dettelees (but if he were wood),
Or live as scarsly as him list desire;
And able for to helpen al a shire
In any caas that mighte falle or happe;
And yet this Manciple sette hir aller cappe.

The REVE was a sclendre colerik man.
His berd was shave as ny as ever he kan; 590
His heer was by his eris ful round yshorn;
His top was dokked lyk a preest biforn.
Ful longe were his legges and ful lene,
Ylik a staf. ther was no calf ysene.
Wel koude he kepe a gerner and a binne;
Ther was noon auditour koude on him winne.
Wel wiste he by the droghte and by the reyn
The yeldinge of his seed and of his greyn.
His lordes sheep, his neet, his dayerie,
His swyn, his hors, his stoor, and his pultrie 600
Was hoolly in this Reves governinge,

69

And by his covenant yaf the rekeninge,
Syn that his lord was twenty yeer of age.
Ther koude no man bringe him in arrerage.
Ther nas baillif, ne hierde, nor oother hine,
That he ne knew his sleighte and his covine;
They were adrad of him as of the deeth.
His woning was ful faire upon an heeth;
With grene trees yshadwed was his place.
610   He koude bettre than his lord purchace.
Ful riche he was astored prively:
His lord wel koude he plesen subtilly,
To yeve and lene him of his owene good,
And have a thank, and yet a cote and hood.
In youthe he hadde lerned a good myster;
He was a wel good wrighte, a carpenter.
This Reve sat upon a ful good stot,
That was al pomely grey and highte Scot.
A long surcote of pers upon he hade,
620   And by his side he baar a rusty blade.
Of Northfolk was this Reve of which I telle,
Biside a toun men clepen Baldeswelle.
Tukked he was as is a frere aboute,
And evere he rood the hindreste of oure route.

A SOMONOUR was ther with us in that place,
That hadde a fyr-reed cherubinnes face,
For saucefleem he was, with eyen narwe.
As hoot he was and lecherous as a sparwe,
With scalled browes blake and piled berd.
630   Of his visage children were aferd.
Ther nas quik-silver, litarge, ne brimstoon,
Boras, ceruce, ne oille of tartre noon;
Ne oinement that wolde clense and bite,

That him mighte helpen of his whelkes white,
Nor of the knobbes sittinge on his chekes.
Wel loved he garleek, oynons, and eek lekes,
And for to drinken strong wyn, reed as blood;
Thanne wolde he speke and crie as he were
     wood.
And whan that he wel dronken hadde the wyn,
Thanne wolde he speke no word but Latin.   640
A fewe termes hadde he, two or thre,
That he had lerned out of som decree—
No wonder is, he herde it al the day;
And eek ye knowen wel how that a jay
Kan clepen 'Watte' as wel as kan the pope.
But whoso koude in oother thing him grope,
Thanne hadde he spent al his philosophie;
Ay '*Questio quid iuris*' wolde he crie.
He was a gentil harlot and a kinde;
A bettre felawe sholde men noght finde.   650
He wolde suffre for a quart of wyn
A good felawe to have his concubyn
A twelf month, and excuse him atte fulle;
Ful prively a finch eek koude he pulle.
And if he foond owher a good felawe,
He wolde techen him to have noon awe
In swich caas of the ercedekenes curs,
But if a mannes soule were in his purs;
For in his purs he sholde ypunisshed be.
'Purs is the ercedekenes helle,' seyde he.   660
But wel I woot he lied right in dede;
Of cursing oghte ech gilty man him drede,
For curs wol slee right as assoilling savith,
And also war him of a *Significavit*.

In daunger hadde he at his owene gise
The yonge girles of the diocise,
And knew hir conseil, and was al hir reed.
A gerland hadde he set upon his heed
As greet as it were for an ale-stake.
670 A bokeleer hadde he maad him of a cake.

    With him ther rood a gentil PARDONER
Of Rouncivale, his freend and his compeer,
That streight was comen fro the court of Rome.
Ful loude he soong 'Com hider, love, to me!'
This Somonour bar to him a stif burdoun;
Was nevere trompe of half so greet a soun.
This Pardoner hadde heer as yelow as wex,
But smothe it heeng as dooth a strike of flex;
By ounces henge his lokkes that he hadde,
680 And therwith he his shuldres overspradde;
But thinne it lay, by colpons oon and oon.
But hood, for jolitee, wered he noon,
For it was trussed up in his walet.
Him thoughte he rood al of the newe jet;
Dischevelee, save his cappe, he rood al bare.
Swiche glaringe eyen hadde he as an hare.
A vernicle hadde he sowed upon his cappe.
His walet lay biforn him in his lappe,
Bretful of pardoun, comen from Rome al hoot.
690 A voys he hadde as smal as hath a goot.
No berd hadde he, ne nevere sholde have;
As smothe it was as it were late shave.
I trowe he were a gelding or a mare.
But of his craft, fro Berwik into Ware,
Ne was ther swich another pardoner.
For in his male he hadde a pilwe-beer,

Which that he seyde was Oure Lady veil:
He seyde he hadde a gobet of the seil
That Seint Peter hadde, whan that he wente
Upon the see, til Jhesu Crist him hente.   700
He hadde a crois of latoun ful of stones,
And in a glas he hadde pigges bones.
But with thise relikes, whan that he fond
A povre person dwellinge upon lond,
Upon a day he gat him moore moneye
Than that the person gat in monthes tweye;
And thus, with feyned flaterie and japes,
He made the person and the peple his apes.
But trewely to tellen atte laste,
He was in chirche a noble ecclesiaste.   710
Wel koude he rede a lessoun or a storie,
But alderbest he song an offertorie;
For wel he wiste, whan that song was songe,
He moste preche and wel affile his tonge
To winne silver, as he ful wel koude;
Therefore he song the murierly and loude.

   Now have I toold you soothly, in a clause,
Th'estaat, th'array, the nombre, and eek the cause
Why that assembled was this compaignie
In Southwerk at this gentil hostelrie   720
That highte the Tabard, faste by the Belle.
But now is time to yow for to telle
How that we baren us that ilke night,
Whan we were in that hostelrie alight;
And after wol I telle of our viage
And al the remenaunt of oure pilgrimage.
But first I pray yow, of youre curteisie,
That ye n'arette it nat my vileynie,

73

Thogh that I pleynly speke in this mateere,
730 To telle yow hir wordes and hir cheere,
Ne thogh I speke hir wordes proprely.
For this ye knowen al so wel as I,
Whoso shal telle a tale after a man,
He moot reherce as ny as evere he kan
Everich a word, if it be in his charge,
Al speke he never so rudeliche and large,
Or ellis he moot telle his tale untrewe,
Or feyne thing, or finde wordes newe.
He may nat spare, althogh he were his brother;
740 He moot as wel seye o word as another.
Crist spak hymself ful brode in hooly writ,
And wel ye woot no vileynie is it.
Eek Plato seith, whoso that kan him rede,
The wordes moote be cosin to the dede.
Also I prey yow to foryeve it me,
Al have I nat set folk in hir degree
Heere in this tale, as that they sholde stonde.
My wit is short, ye may wel understonde.
    Greet chiere made oure Hoost us everichon,
750 And to the soper sette he us anon.
He served us with vitaille at the beste;
Strong was the wyn, and wel to drinke us leste.
A semely man OURE HOOSTE was withalle
For to han been a marchal in an halle.
A large man he was with eyen stepe—
A fairer burgeys is ther noon in Chepe—
Boold of his speche, and wys, and wel ytaught,
And of manhod him lakkede right naught.
Eek therto he was right a mirie man,
760 And after soper pleyen he bigan,

And spak of mirthe amonges othere thinges,
Whan that we hadde maad oure rekeninges,
And seyde thus: 'Now, lordinges, trewely,
Ye been to me right welcome, hertely;
For by my trouthe, if that I shal nat lie,
I saugh nat this yeer so mirie a compaignie
Atones in this herberwe as is now.
Fain wolde I doon yow mirthe, wiste I how.
And of a mirthe I am right now bithoght,
To doon yow ese, and it shal coste noght.   770

    Ye goon to Caunterbury—God yow speede,
The blisful martir quite yow youre meede!
And wel I woot, as ye goon by the weye,
Ye shapen yow to talen and to pleye;
For trewely, confort ne mirthe is noon
To ride by the weye doumb as a stoon;
And therfore wol I maken yow disport,
As I seyde erst, and doon yow som confort.
And if yow liketh alle by oon assent
For to stonden at my juggement,   780
And for to werken as I shal yow seye,
To-morwe, whan ye riden by the weye,
Now, by my fader soule that is deed,
But ye be mirie, I wol yeve yow myn heed!
Hoold up youre hondes, withouten moore speche.'

    Oure conseil was nat longe for to seche.
Us thoughte it was noght worth to make it wys,
And graunted him withouten moore avys,
And bad him seye his voirdit as him leste.
'Lordinges,' quod he, 'now herkneth for the   790
    beste;
But taak it nought, I prey yow, in desdeyn.

This is the point, to speken short and pleyn,
That ech of yow, to shorte with oure weye,
In this viage shal telle tales tweye
To Caunterbury-ward, I mene it so,
And homward he shal tellen othere two,
Of aventures that whilom han bifalle.
And which of yow that bereth him best of alle,
That is to seyn, that telleth in this caas
800   Tales of best sentence and moost solaas,
Shal have a soper at oure aller cost
Heere in this place, sittinge by this post,
Whan that we come again fro Caunterbury.
And for to make yow the moore mury,
I wol myselven goodly with yow ride,
Right at myn owene cost, and be youre gide;
And whoso wole my juggement withseye
Shal paye al that we spenden by the weye.
And if ye vouche sauf that it be so,
810   Tel me anon, withouten wordes mo,
And I wol erly shape me therfore.'
    This thing was graunted, and oure othes
       swore
With ful glad herte, and preyden him also
That he wolde vouche sauf for to do so,
And that he wolde been oure governour,
And of oure tales juge and reportour,
And sette a soper at a certeyn prys,
And we wol reuled been at his devys
In heigh and lough; and thus by oon assent
820   We been acorded to his juggement.
And therupon the wyn was fet anon;
We dronken, and to reste wente echon,

Withouten any lenger taryinge.
    Amorwe, whan that day bigan to springe,
Up roos oure Hoost, and was oure aller cok,
And gadrede us togidre alle in a flok,
And forth we riden a litel moore than paas
Unto the wateringe of Seint Thomas;
And there oure Hoost bigan his hors areste
And seyde, 'Lordinges, herkneth, if yow leste.   830
Ye woot youre foreward, and I it yow recorde.
If even-song and morwe-song accorde,
Lat se now who shal telle the firste tale.
As evere mote I drinke wyn or ale,
Whoso be rebel to my juggement
Shal paye for al that by the wey is spent.
Now draweth cut, er that we ferrer twinne;
He which that hath the shorteste shal biginne.
Sire Knight,' quod he, 'my maister and my
        lord,
Now draweth cut, for that is myn accord.   840
Cometh neer,' quod he, 'my lady Prioresse.
And ye, sire Clerk, lat be youre shamefastnesse,
Ne studieth noght; ley hond to, every man!'
Anon to drawen every wight bigan,
And shortly for to tellen as it was,
Were it by aventure, or sort, or cas,
The sothe is this, the cut fil to the Knight,
Of which ful blithe and glad was every wight,
And telle he moste his tale, as was resoun,
By foreward and by composicioun,   850
As ye han herd; what nedeth wordes mo?
And whan this goode man saugh that it was so,
As he that wys was and obedient

To kepe his foreward by his free assent,
He seyde, 'Sin I shal biginne the game,
What, welcome be the cut, a Goddes name!
Now lat us ride, and herkneth what I seye.'
And with that word we riden forth oure weye,
And he bigan with right a mirie cheere
860 His tale anon, and seyde as ye may heere.

NOTES

4. *of which vertu engendred is the flour* 'whose creative influence brings flowers into blossom'.

5. *Zephirus* The warm west wind; here a generative force.

8. *the Ram* Technically, the zodiacal sign of Aries, through whose 'house'—a twelfth part of the heavens—the sun passes between the middle of March and the middle of April. (For a fuller explanation see *An Introduction to Chaucer*, ch. 6.) In the prologue to *The Man of Law's Tale* the narrator gives the date as 18 April. The ram, a symbol of sexual potency, adds to the sense of a vital process at work in the countryside.

10. *that slepen al the night with open ye* Probably referring to the nightingale, which during the mating season was supposed to sing without interruption for fifteen days. Compare line 98 below.

11. *so priketh hem nature in hir corages* 'so strongly are they moved by natural impulse'.

12. *thanne longen folk to goon on pilgrimages* The long opening sentence reaches its deliberately withheld climax—a satirical suggestion that religious pilgrimages are one of the rites of spring, the result of sap rising in the human plant.

13. *palmeres* Pilgrims who wore a palm-leaf or branch in their hats, in token of having visited the Holy Land.

17. *the hooly blisful martir* Thomas à Becket, Archbishop of Canterbury, who was murdered in the cathedral in 1170 at the instigation of Henry II, and canonized three years later. In 1220 his tomb was opened, and the relics of the martyred archbishop were placed in a coffer overlaid with plates of gold, and set at the base of a shrine in one of the chapels of the cathedral. One end of the coffer was glazed, to allow the faithful to glimpse the relics on the great religious occasions when the canopy covering the feretrum, or chest, was raised. The circumstances of the martyrdom made the shrine of St Thomas one of the most famous centres of Christian pilgrimage. At the jubilee of 1420, according to report, the cathedral was visited by over a hundred thousand pilgrims. Among the other relics offered to view were the bed of the Virgin Mary, fragments of Christ's manger, a piece of rock from Calvary, and Aaron's rod.

18. *that hem hath holpen* 'who has cured them'. The base of the shrine, about six feet high, had three arched recesses on each of its four sides, in which the sick could crouch in hope of being miraculously cured.

20. *in Southwerk at the Tabard* Southwark is a suburb of London immediately south of London Bridge. In Chaucer's lifetime there was no other city bridge across the Thames, and all southbound traffic passed through Southwark. The Tabard was an actual inn, which continued to do business until it was destroyed by fire in 1676. A tabard was a sleeveless jacket or coat, open on both sides, commonly worn by heralds and by noblemen during military campaigns.

22. *with ful devout corage* 'in great piety of spirit'.

24. *wel nine and twenty* 'exactly twenty-nine'. As noted in the Introduction, the company actually numbers thirty.

29. *esed atte beste* 'made very comfortable'.

32. *of hir felaweship* 'accepted as a member of their company'. Numbers strengthened a body of pilgrims against attack by robbers.

33. *made forward* 'agreed'.

37. *me thinketh it acordaunt to resoun* 'it seems to me a logical arrangement'.

39. *so as it semed me* 'as it appeared to me'.

40. *of what degree* 'of what social rank'.

THE KNIGHT ranks above the other pilgrims in the social scale. Chaucer begins appropriately by describing him, and later arranges that the Knight shall tell the first story. He has a more important reason for putting the Knight first. Although on the surface Chaucer seems not much concerned with moral issues, his examination of the pilgrims—and through them of his own society—is directed by a conscious sense of the standards which should determine private and professional behaviour. The Knight who loves 'trouthe and honour, fredom and curteisie', the Parson who spends himself tirelessly in the humble service of Christian ideals, and the Plowman who honours the same principles by his selfless labour in the fields, embody the moral order which holds society together. By beginning with the Knight, Chaucer opens his survey with an outstanding example of human goodness, by whom the moral worth of the other pilgrims can be measured.

The first three pilgrims—the Knight, his attendant Squire

and his Yeoman—form a small group whom Chaucer describes with sober respect. His satirical purpose does not appear until he reaches the fourth pilgrim, the Prioress. By this time the reader has become accustomed to the tone of admiring approval which runs through the three previous portraits, and may not immediately recognize the irony that now underlies Chaucer's effusive compliments. Throughout the *General Prologue* the reader has to be on his guard against Chaucer's seeming enthusiasm towards each of his pilgrims, realizing that his satire operates obliquely through praise that is characteristically lavish and unstinted, whether sincere or not. The summary,

He was a verray, parfit gentil knight   (72)

is straightforwardly respectful, but Chaucer's generous tribute to the Monk,

A manly man, to been an abbot able,   (167)

should leave us wondering whether he means that most abbots were appointed for their worldliness and self-indulgence. When he rounds off the description of the Merchant by remarking,

For sothe he was a worthy man with alle   (285)

Chaucer's irony is obvious, for he has just disclosed the pilgrim's dishonesty and hypocritical manner. Similarly, that 'verray, parfit praktisour' the Physician, although described in terms which recall the Knight, observes a code which inverts the standards of truth, honour and liberality which the Knight strives to uphold. Here Chaucer's seeming praise is doubly ironic. The Physician is not the genuine, perfect practitioner of a noble ideal but shrewd, miserly and self-regarding. In this, Chaucer realistically implies, he is entirely typical of his profession; and thus after all the description is just.

There is nothing equivocal about the portrait of the Knight. His long history of campaigning in crusading wars far from England represents the form of active Christian life which he has pursued since he attained to knighthood. His politeness, modesty and piety build up an impression of virtuous character which is confirmed by his 'bismotered harbergeon'. Unlike the other pilgrims, the Knight has not put on fine clothes for a holiday excursion, but travels in the stained tunic which he has worn in his crusading wars, as though for him the pilgrimage is merely a brief interval between campaigns. Chaucer provides no other detail of the Knight's physical appearance. For this reason his account of the Knight is less immediately striking than that of the Monk or the Wife of Bath, and the picture much less concrete. This is also true of the Parson and of the Plowman. But by giving other pilgrims their vivid concreteness, Chaucer suggests the strength of their physical appetites and the worldliness of their interests. The Knight, like the two other figures of the Christian ideal, shapes his life by an exalted standard which separates him from the materialistic temper of his age. The style of the portrait reflects this difference.

45. *to riden out* 'to take part in military campaigns'.

45–6. *chivalrie, trouthe and honour, freedom and curteisie* 'prowess as a fighting-man respecting the decencies of warfare; steadfastness, loyalty, constancy to his undertakings; honourable behaviour and speech; magnanimity, generosity of mind and purse; gentle manners and unselfish concern for others. The five terms are too complex to be closely defined in a general context such as this. Together they provide a moral touchstone by which the failings of other pilgrims— shiftiness, hypocrisy, self-interest, meanness, vulgarity—are silently measured.

47. *his lordes werre* 'his lord's wars'. Under the feudal system, a knight was bound to render service upon demand to his magnate or overlord. The phrase 'his lordes werre' can have a second sense, since the Knight had been fighting on behalf of his Christian faith.

51, 58. *Alisaundre, Lyeys, Satalie* Chaucer must be referring to the crusading activities of King Peter of Cyprus, who led an expedition against the infidels in 1365 and sacked Alexandria. He had previously harried the Turks in Anatolia, capturing Attalia (Satalie) in 1361, and was subsequently to make raids on the Armenian coast, during one of which he reduced the city of Lyas. In the summer of 1363 he spent about a month in London, gathering support for the coming crusade, and was generously treated by Edward III. Chaucer was in the service either of Lionel or of the king at that time, and so probably saw the royal visitor. There is a short reference to 'worthy Petro, king of Cipre.... That Alisandre wan by heigh maistrie', in *The Monk's Tale*.

52. *he hadde the bord bigonne* 'he had presided at table'.

54. *Lettow, Ruce* 'Lithuania, Russia'.

Notes

55. *no Cristen man so ofte* The reference to religion is explained by the fact that these were wars against heathen peoples. Lithuania became Christian in 1386.

56. *Gernade* Granada in Spain. Algezir was captured in 1344. From Spain the Knight seems to have gone south to Benmarin (Belmarie) in Morocco, and then to Tlemcen (Tramissene, line 62) in Algeria.

58. *Lyeys* Lyas in Armenia; attacked by Peter of Cyprus in 1367 after capturing Attalia (Satalie) in 1361.

59. *the Grete See* The Mediterranean.

63. *in listes* 'in the lists', an enclosure designed for knightly tournaments and armed combat.

65. *the Lord of Palatie* The ruler of Balat in Turkey, who although heathen was allied by treaty to Peter of Cyprus.

68. *wys* 'prudent'; brave, but not a mere hothead.

69. *of his port as meeke as is a maide* 'behaving himself modestly, not forcing himself upon attention'.

70. *nevere yet no vileynie ne saide* 'he had never spoken evil', either gossip or foul language. The term comes from *villein*, a low-born or ignoble person. Compare this aspect of the Knight's character with the Miller's conversation, which was 'moost of sinne and harlotries'. Several of the pilgrims are strongly characterized by their habits of speech: the Merchant, who is 'sowninge alwey th'encrees of his winning'; the Friar, who affected a lisp 'to make his Englissh sweete upon his tonge'; and the Wife, who 'wel koude laughe and carpe'. Chaucer seems to feel most respect for those who speak sparingly and to the point, like the Clerk—'Noght o word spak he moore than was neede'—and the Host, or who discipline their tongues, like the Parson and the Knight. The uncommunicative Reeve, isolated and mistrustful, is repellent in his cold silence.

71. *no maner wight* 'not to any kind or class of person'.

72. *a verray, parfit gentil knight* 'a true and perfect knightly gentleman'. The term 'gentil' implies the noble, generous and courteous qualities appropriate to high birth; honourable and distinguished. Like the less emphatic term 'worthy', it is later applied ironically to pilgrims who have none of these characteristics: the Manciple, the Summoner and the Pardoner. The adjective *verray* is from the French *vrai*, true, and does not correspond with the modern 'very', whose sense is supplied by *ful*.

73. *for to tellen* 'to tell'.

74. *his hors were goode* The Knight had fine horses, but was himself a sombre figure. 'Hors' is the Old English plural form.

75-7. The Knight's fustian tunic is marked with grease and rust from the coat of mail which, until recently, he had worn over it. This graphic touch of description suggests that the Knight had sworn to go on pilgrimage if he returned safely from his last campaign, and that he honours his oath so promptly that he is still in his campaigning dress.

THE SQUIRE. In the Middle Ages a knight was a man of noble birth who had been raised to the rank of knighthood by the king, after serving an apprenticeship as page and squire. These stages of apprenticeship were required as a preliminary to knighthood, even when the aspirant was of noble rank. Chaucer's Squire is qualifying himself for knighthood as an attendant on his own father, and thus their relationship has a double significance. In human terms, it is an association of the carefree gaiety of a young man, still unmarked by experience, with the hardened maturity of middle-age; the Knight's stained and battle-worn tunic offering an eloquent contrast with his son's embroidered finery. Chaucer's comment on the older man, 'he was nat gay' alludes almost pointedly to the quality now lost by the Knight, but springing up again in his son. As a man whose youth is long past, the Knight devotes all his energy to warfare, where the Squire divides his attention between military and courtly accomplishments; proving himself both a courageous soldier and a devoted lover, able to dance, to compose and to play music, and perhaps to write verses. The description of his physical appearance, more detailed than the Knight's, is brought to life by one of the impulsive, emphatic statements which summarize the whole individuality of the pilgrim:

> He was as fressh as is the month of May. (92)

Chaucer is beginning to disclose a second standard of judgement, not ethical but natural: an approval of healthy vitality and self-confidence, which he sees represented in the 'fresshe floures, white and reede' that decorate the Squire's short gown.

80. *bacheler* Not in a matrimonial sense, though the Squire is unmarried, but—like a Bachelor of Arts—a probationer for a final degree or honour; perhaps that of courtesy as well as of knighthood.

81. *as they were leyd in presse* 'as if artificially curled'.
83. *of evene lengthe* 'moderately tall'.
86. *Flaundres, Artois, Picardie* Districts of northern France. As a young man, Chaucer himself had seen military service in this area. The Squire might have taken part in the so-called crusade led by the Bishop of Norwich to this region in 1383.
87. *as of so litel space* 'in such a comparatively short while'.
88. *in hope to stonden in his lady grace* 'in the hope of winning the favour or respect of his lady', who might then consent to accept him as her servant. The noun 'lady' belongs to an Old English weak declension whose genitive form is unchanged.
89. *embrouded was he, as it were a meede* 'his clothes were embroidered like a meadow'. Chaucer appears to have borrowed several ideas for the Squire from the portrait of Mirth in the *Roman de la Rose*, part of which he translated. Like the Squire, Mirthe is 'delyver, smert (agile), and of gret myght' (compare line 84), is young, tall and handsome, and richly dressed, 'in samet, with briddes wrought'. The Squire's gaiety, described in line 91, brings to life a comment in the *Roman*, 'Ne sawe thou nevere man so lyght'. Both figures have curly hair and express a taste for showy dress, Mirthe wearing a robe 'al toslytered for queyntise'; slashed in fashionable style. Unlike Mirthe, the Squire is more than a symbolic figure of youthful vigour and lightheartedness; but the particular character which Chaucer gives him—and perhaps his technique of character-drawing generally—owes a good deal to suggestions developed from the much earlier French poem.
93. *short was his gowne* A fashion designed to show the elegance of a young man's legs. The 'sleves longe and wide', on the other hand, might reach nearly to the floor.
95–6. *he koude songes make . . . and weel purtreye and write* 'he was adept at composing songs and verses, at jousting and dancing, and could draw and write gracefully'.
99. *lowely and servisable* 'modest and selfless in carrying out his duties'. These two qualities set the stamp of moral approval upon the Squire. They are shared by the Knight, the Parson and the Plowman, each of whom disregards personal comfort in serving an ideal. Most of the other pilgrims think only of enriching themselves, or of enjoying the material pleasures of the world.
100. *and carf biforn his fader* Like the squire in *The Merchant's Tale*, who 'carf biforn the knight ful many a day'; line 528. Carving formed one of the regular duties of a squire, probably

as a means of assuring that his master was served with food
befitting his rank.

The group is completed by THE YEOMAN, who acts as personal
bodyguard to his master the Knight. He is a countryman, who
when not serving his feudal lord as now, would be carrying out
the duties of a forester, preserving vert and venison—the deer
and the green vegetation which provides cover for them—in one
of the royal forests. The Yeoman is not one of the important
pilgrims, for no tale is allotted to him and Chaucer does not
refer to him again; but these fifteen lines provide the first
extended example of Chaucer's power of visual suggestion. The
single comment, 'A not heed hadde he, with a broun visage',
brings the man graphically before us, three successive aspirates,
'heed hadde he', suggesting an oak-like toughness of physique
and of spirit. Characteristic touches of emphasis, 'bright and
kene', 'a mighty bowe', 'sharp as point of spere', and the
flashes of colour and polished metal about the Yeoman complete
an impression of lively vigour and alertness. Chaucer says
nothing about his moral character. As a man spending his life
in close contact with the natural world, the Yeoman seems not
to follow any consciously formulated code of behaviour, but to
respect instinctive principles as simple and sturdily dependable
as himself. He is revealed by his loyal service and the fighting
trim of his professional equipment; a man unaffected by the
ambition and greed of urban society and humanly fulfilled in the
conscientious performance of his duties.

102. *for him liste* 'since it pleased him'. The Knight is being
referred to. His willingness to travel with a single attendant
is another mark of his modesty.

104. *pecok arwes* 'arrows feathered with peacock plumage'.

106. *wel koude he dresse his takel yemanly* 'he knew how to look
after his equipment very capably'.

107. *his arwes drouped noght* Feathers should stand out stiffly
from the shaft. If they do not, the arrow will not fly true, and
will drop short of the target.

109. *a broun visage* The effect of his open-air life, like the
Shipman whom 'the hoote somer hadde maad...al broun'
(line 396).

110. *of wodecrafte wel koude he al the usage* 'he knew all there
was to know about the customs and practices of woodcraft'—
in particular, probably, those relating to the chase.

115. *a Christopher* A medallion of St Christopher, patron saint of foresters and of travellers.
116. *an horn* Used to signal stages in the progress of a hunt.

THE PRIORESS. The ruminative final line of the Yeoman's description lowers the intensity of the writing and provides a quiet transition to the first of the female pilgrims. Almost immediately, with the innocent disclosure that the Prioress had taken the name not of a saint but of a heroine of courtly romance, the seriously respectful attitude which Chaucer has maintained so far dissolves, and reveals the impish satirical purpose beneath. Pretending not to realize the significance of what he observes, he shows us a woman whose real interests lie not with her religious vocation but in the fashionable world, which she knows only by hearsay. She tries to adopt the manners of a courtly lady but succeeds only in appearing genteel and over-refined among the other pilgrims, who are, perhaps, rather awed by her delicate behaviour. Chaucer sees the nun in Madame Eglentine as a charming imposture, imperfectly concealing a woman whose social ambitions lead her into an absurd confusion of purposes—a mimicking of courtly mannerisms that are completely inappropriate to her calling. Whether the portrait directs any deliberate satire against the Church is not certain. The Prioress was violating an ecclesiastical edict by going on pilgrimage. Her pet dogs were also forbidden, her fine forehead should have been veiled, and probably her wimple should have been not fluted but plain. This disregard for the rules of her order is matched by the Monk's open contempt in lines 175–87 for the edicts of St Augustine, and may represent a conscious criticism of the corrupt state of the Church at the time. But perhaps the rules which the Prioress violates were so frequently ignored that Chaucer felt less concern for her actual misdeeds than for the comic incongruity which they reveal. In common with other poets—Shakespeare conspicuous among them—Chaucer shows himself to be fascinated by the disparity between what is and what seems to be. His irony exploits this kind of disparity by putting forward disrespectful comments in the disguise of approving observations.

119. *hir smiling was ful simple and coy* Chaucer begins by referring to the least expected attribute of a nun. Her expression should have been sober and withdrawn, perhaps even for-

bidding. The phrase 'ful simple' suggests cultivated artlessness rather than unaffected simplicity.

120. *Seinte Loy* St Eligius or Eloi, who had a reputation for personal beauty and courtesy. It was contrary to the rules of the Prioress's order to swear at all, but as St Eloi himself refused to swear, to swear by him was considered a 'white' oath.

121. *Eglentine* A nun usually adopts the name of a female saint or of a virtue. The Prioress takes the name of a wild rose, also used of a heroine of a romance tale.

123. *entuned in hir nose ful semely* 'intoned through her nose most attractively'. The habit was fashionable at the time, but 'semely' is ironic. The term also means fitting, appropriate, and in the nunnery such fashionable behaviour is badly out of place.

124. *and Frenssh she spak* Here again Chaucer is praising the Prioress for an accomplishment which might distinguish a courtly lady, but which has no place in the cloister. The admiring tone of the remark encourages us to overlook the irrelevance of the Prioress's talent.

125. *after the scole of Stratford atte Bowe* 'according to the fashion of the Benedictine nunnery at Bromley in Middlesex', whose inmates appear to have been recruited from the less distinguished ranks of society. The Prioress airs her French in order to suggest that she has an aristocratic background, and—without realizing it—gives herself away by that very device. French had been the language of the court since the Norman Conquest.

127. *at mete wel ytaught was she* the observations which follow show that the Prioress had made a careful study of table-manners and etiquette in contemporary writings, and that she is carrying out their instructions to the letter. Chaucer is continuing to admire her for qualities which have no bearing on her religious capacity.

129. *ne wette hir fingres* table-forks were not introduced until the end of the sixteenth century. In Chaucer's lifetime food was carried to the mouth in the fingers.

132. *in curteisie was set ful muchel hir lest* 'she had the greatest regard for politeness and good manners'.

134-5. *ther was no ferthing sene of grece* 'she left no spot of grease from her lips floating in the cup'.

136. *ful semely after hir mete she raughte* 'she reached for her food decorously', without straining or grabbing. The main

dishes stood in the centre of the table, the guests helping themselves to portions. The adverb 'semely' is used three times in the description of the Prioress (lines 123, 136 and 151); a keyword to character which Chaucer is building up.

137. *of greet desport* 'very merry'; recalling the 'smiling' of line 119.

138. *amiable of port* 'friendly': again hardly suitable to her calling.

139–40. *peyned hire to countrefete cheere of court* 'was at pains to imitate courtly manners and appearance'.

141. *to ben holden digne of reverence* 'to be considered worthy of respect'. In her friendliness and readiness to be amused, the Prioress does not unbend far enough to lose sight of her dignity, whether as mother-superior or as a lady.

142. *conscience* Besides having its modern sense, the term meant tender-heartedness and sensitive feeling. The immediate context, 'so charitable and so pitous', suggests that Chaucer intends the first meaning, but the examples of 'conscience' which follow in lines 144–9 disclose his ironic purpose. The delicate feelings and sympathies of a would-be courtly lady replace the spiritual consciousness that would be expected of a Prioress.

147. *rosted flessh, or milk and wastel-breed* The 'povre widwe' of the *Nun's Priest's Tale* subsists on a much more frugal diet. This pampering of lapdogs shows how badly the Prioress's charity and pity are misdirected.

154. *a fair forheed* Like the small red mouth and grey-blue eyes which the Prioress is fortunate to possess, a broad forehead was much esteemed as a mark of beauty. Immodestly, the Prioress lets it be seen.

156. *nat undergrowe* 'not under-developed', but a well-shaped woman whose behaviour allows Chaucer to become aware of her physical attractiveness.

159. *a peire of bedes* 'a rosary'; a string of beads used in reciting prayers, whose larger beads—representing Paternosters and Glorias—separated runs of ten smaller beads representing Aves, prayers to the Virgin Mary. The 'gauds' or Paternoster beads in this particular rosary are green, the Ave beads of red coral. The effect would be highly decorative, and not immediately suggestive of piety. Rosaries are usually black.

160. *ful sheene* 'bright and shining', as metallic objects invariably are for Chaucer.

162. *amor vincit omnia* 'love conquers all things'. The motto applies ambiguously to sacred and to profane love.

163. *another Nonne* she subsequently tells the tale of 'the lyf of Seinte Cecile' without herself being described.

164. *hir chapeleyne* or capellana, a kind of private secretary and assistant.

and preestes thre only one of these, the Nun's Priest, is subsequently heard of. It has been objected that the Prioress would not need more than one such attendant, and that the inclusion of two superfluous priests could explain why Chaucer's nine-and-twenty does not tally with the count of heads. One suggestion is that Chaucer left the line unfinished, intending to insert a description of the second Nun, and that the phrase 'and preestes thre' was added by another hand. If so, the Nun's Priest was not to be mentioned at all in the *General Prologue*. The phrase has to be accepted as it stands, as a point which Chaucer had not properly resolved.

The Prioress is followed by a second ecclesiastical pilgrim, THE MONK. Monks were members of a religious community, vowed to poverty, chastity and obedience, and living apart from the world. The monastery with its adjoining fields and gardens supplied all the material wants of its inmates, who were able to serve God and sanctify themselves in a life uninterrupted by the cares of normal human existence. The monastic day, spent for the most part in silence, was divided between prayer, meditation and study, and in manual labour or some simple craft. The portrait of Chaucer's Monk suggests how far this unworldly ideal had become lost by the end of the fourteenth century. Like the Prioress, he is out of sympathy with the ascetic rule of his monastic order. He declares himself uncompromisingly for 'the newe world' and dismisses the edicts of its founder in contempt: 'He yaf nat of that text a pulled hen', and, 'Thilke text heeld he nat worth an oystre'. From first to last he proves himself a man of the world, relishing the pleasures of good food, expensive clothing, recreation and freedom, and arguing vigorously that the restrictions of monastic life are now outmoded. 'How shal the world be served?' he demands, meaning that secular affairs cannot be carried on without the help of the educated and capable men who are bottled up inside the cloister. The point escapes him that monasteries were built to protect their inmates from the distracting affairs outside, and with the object of serving not the world but God. Chaucer takes up the point quietly, pretending to be impressed by the Monk's loquacity as by his splendid clothes and mount. His admiration is not entirely insincere. As a priest and a monastic recluse the Monk is a complete failure, dominated by a love of luxury and pleasure, but Chaucer recognizes that he is 'a manly man', whose physical energy and liveliness are unmistakably shown by his shining complexion, bright eyes, and eagerness for open-air activities. The poet's moral disapproval is tempered by this proof of the Monk's sparkling vitality, and the joyousness of his response to life.

165. *a fair for the maistrie* 'surpassing all others'.
166. *an outridere* A monk entrusted with the care of monastic estates, which took him outside the cloister.
167. *an abbot* The head of an abbey, as a prior or prioress is head of a priory, the subordinate house of an abbey.
169. *his bridel...ginglen* Bells were commonly fixed to medieval bridles or harness. Chaucer's simile is wryly ironic, for the Monk's chapel-bell is not loud enough to make itself heard through this jingling.
172. *ther as this lord was kepere of the celle* 'in the subordinate monastic house where this Monk was in charge'.
173. *the reule of seint Maure* St Maurus, a disciple of St Benedict—'seint Beneit'—established monasticism in Europe in 529, by founding the order of Benedictines at Monte Cassino. The Rule of St Benedict was the code of monastic life whose main points are summarized in the head-note above. It was adopted by all the subsequent monastic orders.
176. *heeld after the newe world the space* 'followed the new fashion'; the pleasure-seeking and self-interest which had replaced the dedicated religious life of the past. The exact sense of 'the space' is uncertain, but appears to be 'for the time being', or 'meanwhile'.
180. *is likned til* 'is comparable with'.
182. *nat worth an oystre* Chaucer uses many similar expressions, which were plentiful in Middle English: the 'pulled hen' of line 177 above, 'nat worth a boterflye', 'rekke nat a bene', 'sette nat an hawe'.
183. *And I seyde his opinion was good* Which clearly it isn't. His irony makes Chaucer appear as impious as the Monk, but

Notes

his pretence of approval is a straight-faced joke which caps the outrageousness of the Monk's argument.

184. *what sholde he* 'why should he'.

185. *upon a book in cloistre alwey to poure* As mentioned above, study formed part of the Benedictine rule. The Benedictines have always been a learned order. The Monk is scornful of this distinction, sharing the Host's lack of respect for scholarship.

187. *as Austin bit* 'as St Augustine commands'.

how shal the world be served? 'how will essential secular duties and offices be performed if the clergy confine themselves to religious observation and manual labour?'

188. *to him reserved* 'kept for himself'.

192. *for no cost wolde he spare* 'he would not give up hunting at any price'.

193–4. *purfiled at the hond with gris* 'trimmed at the wrist with costly grey fur'. The rule of his order permitted the Monk only a plain habit and cowl.

194. *of a lond* 'in the land'.

196. *a ful curious pin* 'a pin very skilfully made'.

197. *a love-knotte* A device in the form of a knot or bow, supposed to be a love-token. Like the Prioress's engraved brooch, this personal adornment—forbidden by the rule—casts some doubt upon the chastity which the Monk has sworn to observe. All the ecclesiastical pilgrims fall under this suspicion except the Parson, who has accepted celibacy like the others.

199. *as he hadde been enoint* 'as though he had been anointed': with an ironic allusion to the religious rite which confers sanctity upon a chosen person.

200. *in good point* = embonpoint, 'stout'.

202. *that stemed as a forneys of a leed* 'that gleamed like a fire under a cauldron'.

203. *in greet estaat* 'in splendid condition'.

205. *a forpined goost* 'the ghost of a man wasted by suffering'.

The four orders of mendicant friars were founded during the thirteenth and fourteenth centuries. Unlike monks, who were supposed to remain within the cloister, friars were licensed to wander about the country preaching and begging money for the support of their friary. Their life was open to obvious abuses. Chaucer's FRIAR is a plausible hypocrite, greedy, snobbish

92

and sexually promiscuous, who misuses confession and neglects the needy for a more profitable association with an easy-living class of affluent merchants and 'worthy women'. By turning confession into a painless business arrangement—tacitly inviting the rich to buy absolution without the discomfort of doing penance—he weakens the authority of the local priest and corrupts one of the great sacraments of the Church. Chaucer treats the Monk and the Prioress with some amused indulgence, recognizing that they do not actively harm the religion whose principles they regard so lightly. But the Friar seems to evoke a sense of outrage which Chaucer voices through a sarcastic commentary on the Friar's cynical exploitation of his faith. It is greed which makes him so successful a beggar, not religious zeal, and his own purse and belly which he is most concerned to fill.

209. *a limitour* A friar licensed to beg within a specified district or limit.

 ful solempne 'dignified and impressive'. The tone of Chaucer's remark, itself 'ful solempne', warns us to handle the comment cautiously.

210. *the ordres foure* Dominicans, Franciscans, Carmelites and Austin Friars, in order of precedence.

211. *daliaunce and fair langage* 'gossip and elegant manner of speech'; see lines 266–7. But the phrase can also mean lovemaking and persuasive argument, empty promises. The next remark confirms the *double entendre*.

213. *at his owene cost* 'out of his own pocket'. The comment suggests that this kind man found husbands for poor girls, either paying the expenses of the wedding or himself providing the bride's dowry, or both. In fact these are girls whom the Friar has seduced, and whom he is marrying off with a bribe to the husband, to avoid open scandal. The sexual laxity of friars is referred to again by the Wife of Bath: see her Prologue and Tale, lines 873–81.

214. *he was a noble post* An entirely ironic remark; 'noble' being as inappropriate as the 'worthy' of line 271.

216. *with frankeleyns* Who, as Chaucer indicates later, enjoyed a reputation for fine living.

218. *he hadde power of confessioun* The Friar was licensed to hear confession. This privilege enabled him to attract the parishioners of the local priest—the *curat* of line 219—by offering easier terms of absolution.

224. *ther as he wiste to have a good pitaunce* Where he knew he could expect a generous gift from the penitent. The modern sense of pittance—a bare sufficiency—represents a considerable change of meaning.

225-32. The whole passage is scathingly ironic. Chaucer repeats with apparent approval the Friar's argument that a generous tip to the confessor—a much more convincing sign of sincere repentance than weeping and praying—proves that the penitent has been truly shriven.

227. *if he yaf, he dorste make avaunt* If a man offered such a gift after confession, the Friar was ready to declare him truly penitent.

234. *pinnes, for to yeven faire wives* In the fourteenth century pins were not always easy to come by.

237. *of yeddinges he baar outrely the prys* 'as a ballad-singer the Friar was quite outstanding'. From lines 236 and 268 it appears that he accompanied himself on the rote, a small harp. His accomplishment would be more praiseworthy in a layman than in a priest.

238. *his nekke whit* This lily-white neck contrasts unfavourably with the healthy tan of the Yeoman and the Shipman.

242. *bet than a lazar or a beggestere* 'he was better acquainted with innkeepers and barmaids than with lepers and female beggars'.

244. *acorded nat, as by his facultee* 'did not befit the dignity of his professional status'. Chaucer sarcastically pretends to agree.

246. *nat honest* 'not respectable or fitting'.
    it may nat avaunce 'there's no profit in it'.

247. *for to deelen with no swich poraille* 'to associate with such poverty-stricken wretches'. The stinging contempt of the remark reveals the uncharitable nature which the Friar conceals from the rich: compare line 250.

248. *selleres of vitaille* 'provision merchants', at whose tables, as at those of franklins, good food could be expected.

249-50. *ther as profit sholde arise, curteis he was and lowely of service* Wherever there was a chance of personal gain, the Friar put on ingratiating and courteous manners. The comment invites comparison with the Squire, who is 'curteis, lowely, and servisable', and with the 'noble ensample' of the Parson's way of life. But these are men of genuine humility, serving without expectation or hope of personal profit.

251. *ther nas no man nowher so vertuous* 'no one could have been more gentlemanly and obliging'. Chaucer is playing on two senses of 'vertuous'.

252. *his hous* 'his friary'. Friars spent most of their time in the world, and used the friary only as an occasional hostel.

253–4. The Friar paid rent—'a certeyn ferme'—for the district in which he was limiter, so obtaining exclusive rights to operate there. These two lines figure in only one manuscript, but their authenticity is not disputed.

255. *hadde noght a sho* 'was extremely poor'; compare the modern phrase, 'without a shirt to his back'.

256. '*In principio*' 'In the beginning': the opening words of St John's gospel, which were regarded with special reverence and even held to possess magical power.

258. *his purchas was wel bettre than his rente* Either (i) 'the income of his begging far exceeded the rent which he paid for his exclusive rights' (lines 253–4 above) or (ii) 'he made much more money than he declared to his friary'.

259. *rage he koude, as it were right a whelp* 'he knew how to frolic like a puppy'.

260. *love-dayes* Days appointed for the friendly solution of quarrels. The Friar's buffoonery helps to put the disputants in good humour. Chaucer is probably referring equivocally to this and to the private 'love-days' hinted at in line 211 above.

262. *a povre scoler* Compare the dress of the Clerk (line 292 below).

263. *a maister* Having a Master's degree, which conferred great dignity upon its recipient.

264. *double worstede* A heavier and more expensive form of worsted, a woollen fabric originally made at Worstead in Norfolk.

semicope Short cope or cape.

265. *rounded as a belle out of the presse* 'shaped as though it came out of a bell-mould'.

266. *for his wantownesse* 'out of affectation'.

267. *sweete upon his tonge* Chaucer's fourth reference to the charming manner of speech which the Friar adopts when it suits his purpose, though not when referring to the 'poraille'.

268. *harping* A much smaller instrument than the modern harp is intended, such as the rote or crowd of line 237.

269. *his eyen twinkled* The simile which follows restores the amiable tone of Chaucer's narrative.

Notes

With THE MERCHANT, Chaucer breaks the sequence of
ecclesiastical figures, by presenting a secular counterpart of the
Friar. He is another outwardly respectable pilgrim, stylishly
dressed and mounted, whose dignified solemnity covers a moral
sham. The Merchant's high saddle and imported beaver hat
characterize his lofty condescension, and also the shakiness of
his financial position. Despite his pompous mode of address
and his constant talk about business profits, the Merchant is a
debtor, struggling to rescue himself from bankruptcy by illegal
transactions in foreign exchange and shady operations as a
usurer. Chaucer sees through the imposture, and puts down
the Merchant's self-important air very firmly, by failing to
remember his name. The effortlessness of the exposure leaves
Chaucer unruffled, and the Merchant unaware that his pretence
of business integrity has been penetrated and laid bare in a few
almost casual comments.

273. *in mottelee* 'dressed in motley', a cloth of mixed colour,
  such as tweed or homespun.
274. *a Flaundrissh bever hat* An imported fur hat of the
  most expensive kind, worn by the Merchant as a prestige
  symbol.
276. *his resons he spak ful solempnely* 'he expressed his opinions
  gravely and seriously'.
277. *sowninge alwey th'encrees of his winning* 'repeatedly men-
  tioning his increasing profits'.
278. *he wolde the see were kept for any thing* 'he wished the sea
  passage between Middelburg and Orwell to be protected
  against pirates at all costs'.
279. *Middelburgh* A port on the island of Walcheren, off the
  coast of Holland, where the Merchant Adventurers were
  established for some years from 1384.
    Orewelle, Orwell, a port on the river between Ipswich and
  Harwich, now defunct. Evidently the Merchant was engaged
  in exporting English cloth to the Low Countries. This was
  the principal activity of the Merchant Venturers, a rich and
  powerful class in fourteenth-century England.
280. *wel koude he in eschaunge sheeldes selle* The remark sounds
  complimentary. In fact the Merchant's dealing in foreign
  exchange—selling French *écus* at a profit—was illegal.
281. *ful wel his wit bisette* 'made good use of his cunning'.
283. *estatly...of his gouvernaunce* 'dignified in his behaviour'.

284. *with his bargaines and with his chevissaunce* 'in his business deals and monetary transactions'. Both terms are ambiguous, financial operations of the kind they describe carrying a strong hint of dishonesty.

285. *A worthy man* Again using the description ironically, as in line 271. The Merchant may be worthy in the sense of being socially eminent, but not in respect of moral character.

286. *I noot how men him calle* 'I don't know his name': as suggested in the head-note above, a calculated snub to the Merchant's haughty self-valuation. There remains a possibility that Chaucer is playing the innocent by pretending not to recognise the man he has described. Such a convention existed in medieval German poetry, where the formula 'Ine weiz' (I don't know) allowed the poet to profess his ignorance of matters familiar to himself and his readers, but better left unsaid. Such a device would certainly have suited Chaucer's comic spirit.

THE CLERK. During the Middle Ages, scholarship—and indeed education—was a virtual monopoly of the Church, and the laity were for the most part illiterate. Most clerks, whom we should call scholars, entered the Church and became 'clerks in holy orders'; still a synonym for priests today. Chaucer's Clerk is one of the few pilgrims not affected by worldly or mercenary ambitions. He is dedicated to the pursuit of knowledge, indifferent to personal comfort and appearance, and too deeply immersed in his studies to join in the scramble for profitable appointments. Unlike the Monk, he ignores the world and its physical attractions, content to go threadbare and dependent upon the alms of his friends so long as he can remain at the university, and perhaps eventually possess a few books. Chaucer acknowledges the Clerk's single-mindedness, his acute intellect and his high moral standards, but without overlooking the element of absurdity in such threadbare poverty and emaciation. In respect of his unworldliness the Clerk might stand beside the Parson, yet the joke,

> But al be that he was a philosophre,
> Yet hadde he but litel gold in cofre   (299–300)

hints at the fruitlessness of the Clerk's passionate absorption in books. The Parson is poor, and content with limited means, but he does not take poverty to such extremes as this. More important, he spends himself actively for others, where the Clerk is shut up in a private world of study which takes no account of his fellow-men. His underfed horse, and his own scarecrow appearance, reveal a man starved of contact with the great concourse of everyday human affairs from which Chaucer brings such a rich harvest.

287. *a clerk...of Oxenford* 'a scholar studying for a degree at Oxford'.

288. *that unto logik hadde longe ygo* 'who had proceeded to logic a long while before'. The medieval study of the arts was divided into two courses; the *trivium*, consisting of grammar, logic and rhetoric, and the *quadrivium*, consisting of arithmetic, geometry, astronomy and music.

290. *he nas nat right fat* 'the Clerk himself was not at all well-nourished'.

291. *and therto sobrely* 'and grave in addition'.

292. *his overeste courtepy* 'his outermost garment', a short coat.

293. *he hadde geten him yet no benefice* As yet the Clerk had not been appointed to an ecclesiastical living, such as a chaplaincy or the cure of a parish.

294. *for to have office* 'to accept secular employment', as a civil servant or diplomat.

295. *him was levere* 'he would rather'. 'Levere' is the comparative of 'leef', meaning dear: thus the literal meaning of the phrase is 'it was more dear to him'.

296. *twenty bookes* Such a private library would represent a considerable outlay of money. Books were at this time manuscript works, as the invention of printing lay still more than half a century ahead.

297. *Aristotle* The greatest of the ancient Greek philosophers, 384 to 322 B.C., whose works on metaphysics, natural science, politics, ethics and religion provided the basis of medieval thought. All Oxford curricula included his study.

299. *but al be that he was a philosophre* 'although he was a philosopher'—that is, a lover of wisdom and truth. The term could be applied to any serious student of the arts. Here there is a play on a second sense of philosopher—an alchemist. The search for the 'philosopher's stone' that would transmute base metals to gold continued throughout the later Middle Ages and beyond. '*Although* he loved knowledge he had little money', is sardonic: one would expect 'because'.

303. *and bisily gan . . . preye* 'and prayed earnestly'. The auxiliary 'gan' has the same function as 'did'.

305. *of studie took he moost cure and moost heede* 'he devoted himself entirely to his studies'.

307. *in forme and reverence* 'with proper formality and respect'.

308. *ful of hy sentence* 'full of meat'; of moral observation, wise judgement and pithy sayings. 'Sentence' is one of the conditions which the Host requires of the tales to be recounted (line 800).

309. *sowninge in moral vertu* 'always inclining towards virtuousness'.

THE MAN OF LAW. The Man of Law exists as an impression of character without realized form. Chaucer describes his professional abilities in some detail but says nothing about his personal appearance, and after only two lines given to the Man of Law's attire breaks off as though he had lost interest in the subject. If, as seems likely, the description is based on the character of a particular Judge of Assize, there would have been good reason for Chaucer's reticence. But this lack of human detail denies the Man of Law the lively individuality given to the Prioress and the Monk by close observation of personal habits or by indirect reporting of speech; and the satirical comment, 'he semed bisier than he was', exposes a private weakness with no attempt at subtlety.

311. *war and wys* 'discreet and discerning'.

312. *at the Parvis* The reference has not been satisfactorily explained. It evidently refers to a meeting-place, either in the porch of St Paul's or at Westminster, where lawyers consulted with their clients in the afternoon, when the courts were closed.

313. *ful riche of excellence* 'a man of exceptional talent and ability'. Effusive praise of this kind in Chaucer generally conceals an ironic purpose.

315. *he semed swich* 'or so it appeared'. Chaucer's disrespectful remark at line 324 admits the irony half-hidden in this remark.

316. *justice he was ful often in assise* 'he frequently acted as judge in the Assize Courts', where criminal cases were heard.

317. *by patente and by pleyn commissioun* 'by letters-patent from the king appointing him judge, and by personal commission

giving him powers of jurisdiction'. About twenty such judges held office at this time. There may be a punning reference to one of them in line 328.

318. *for his science* 'through his legal expertise'.

319. *of fees and robes hadde he many oon* Referring to the legal expression *foeda et robae*, and meaning that the Man of Law was of the livery of several magnates for whom he did useful service.

320. *so greet a purchasour* 'such a great buyer of land', presumably on behalf of the client for whom he drew up the deed of conveyance, after converting complicated tenures into freehold.

321. *al was fee simple to him* Punning on the legal term 'fee simple', which means absolute possession, and the easy money which the Man of Law made by his practice.

322. *his purchasing mighte nat been infect* 'there could be no legal dispute over the ownership of property whose title-deeds he had drawn up'.

325–6. 'he was closely familiar with all the legal cases and judgements since the Norman Conquest'.

327. *therto he koude endite* 'in addition he knew how to draw up legal documents'.

328. *ther koude no wight pinche at his writing* Meaning that he left no loophole in the deed by which its validity might be challenged. Chaucer may be punning on the name of a justice of Common Pleas, Thomas Pinchbek, who signed a writ for the poet's arrest for a small debt in 1388.

329. *koude he pleyn by rote* 'he knew by heart from beginning to end'.

330. *but hoomly* 'informally', not as though he were on circuit as a judge.

   medlee 'medley'; cloth of mixed colour, similar to motley.

331. *barres smale* 'narrow stripes'.

THE FRANKLIN. This class of freeholder or landowner ranked next below the gentry in Chaucer's society, and appears from the allusion in line 216 of the *General Prologue* to have enjoyed a reputation for hospitality and good living. The comment, 'an housholdere, and that a greet, was he', shows that Chaucer's Franklin was a man of substance who could properly represent his county in Parliament.

In this portrait Chaucer returns to the infectious gaiety of mood in which he describes the Squire. The Franklin is one of the happiest of the pilgrims, a man finding endless delight in the pleasures of fine cooking and lavish hospitality, and radiating a spirit of content. 'It snewed in his hous of mete and drinke', Chaucer asserts, and as though disarmed by such unstinting generosity he offers no openly critical comment on the Franklin. By associating him with the daisy—a flower for which, in *The Legend of Good Women*, Chaucer admits 'so gret affeccioun'— the poet makes a mark of approval confirmed in a series of unqualified compliments. The Franklin's high living does not imply gluttony, nor that he is neglecting more important issues in his enthusiasm for the pleasures of the table. Its well-stocked cellars, its incomparable bread and ale, its ready supply of fat partridges and bream and its flavoursome dishes changing with the seasons, make the house rival the abundance of the natural world, with the Franklin presiding over the feast as though it were an everlasting harvest-home. Yet it is hard to believe that Chaucer's critical discernment is entirely suspended, or that the man who shows such respect for the self-abnegating spirit of the Knight and the Parson regards the Franklin's epicurean life with complete approval. If Chaucer intends any ironic criticism, it must be expressed through what is not said—in the absence of moral or spiritual purpose to offset the Franklin's dedication to the pleasures of food and wine.

335. *of his complexioun he was sangwin* 'he was sanguine in temperament'—one of the four human types recognized by medieval physiology. The others are choleric, phlegmatic and melancholy. A sanguine complexion—indicated by a red face—was accounted superior to the other three, and supposed to be accompanied by comeliness of body, amiability and cheerfulness. (For a more detailed explanation see *An Introduction to Chaucer*, ch. 6.)

336. *by the morwe* 'to start the day'.
a sop in wyn 'a piece of spiced bread dipped in wine'.

338. *Epicurus* An Athenian philosopher of the third century B.C., who came to be regarded as the patron of sensual pleasures.

339–40. *that pleyn delit was verray felicitee parfit* 'that gratification of the senses constituted the highest form of pleasure'. In fact Epicurus identified pleasure with the practice of virtue, but his followers isolated his belief that the highest good was pleasure and made this their excuse for self-indulgence. Chaucer's seeming approval of the Franklin's creed is open to doubt.

341. *an housholdere* The owner, as distinct from the tenant, of a house, and the family head.

342. *Seint Julian* Patron saint of hospitality.

343. *after oon* 'uniformly good'.

344. *a bettre envined man was nowher noon* 'nowhere was there a man who kept a better-stocked cellar'.

345. *bake meat...of fissh and flessh* 'meat pie, or fish pie'.

347. *it snewed in his hous of mete and drinke* Snowing suggests winter and scarcity, but in the Franklin's house it is a season of abundance.

349. *after the sondry sesons of the yeer* 'in accordance with the time of year'.

352. *luce in stuwe* 'pike in his pond'. Castles and great houses had fishponds in which fish could be kept alive until required for eating.

353. *wo was his cook but if* 'his cook was in serious trouble unless...'.

354. *redy al his geere* 'all his cooking utensils ready for use'.

355. *table dormant* A table fixed to the floor, and so permanent. Trestle tables, dismantled after meals, were much more usual in medieval houses.

   in his halle The main room of the house, in which—as in the colleges of Oxford and Cambridge—the communal meal was served.

356. *redy covered* 'with cloth spread', ready for a meal.

357. *at sessiouns ther was he lord and sire* 'he presided over sessions of magistrates', at which petty offenders were tried.

358. *knight of the shire* 'member of Parliament for his county'. Chaucer was appointed Knight of the Shire for Kent in 1386.

360. *whit as morne milk* Before the cream has risen to the top. The Franklin is associated with this colour three times.

361. *shirreve...and countour* 'sheriff and county auditor'. The sheriff represented royal authority in his shire, and was responsible for law and order.

THE FIVE GILDSMEN. None of the members of this little group appears again, and it has been supposed that Chaucer added them as an afterthought. By separating the Franklin and the Cook, they interrupt a long recital of culinary matters which otherwise might have become wearisome. These eighteen lines show Chaucer being mischievously ironic at the expense of small-town vanity and self-importance. Seen from the court, the struggles of gildsmen's wives over precedence appear merely lilliputian, and their husbands' 'solempne and greet fraternitee' shrinks to a social gild that seems important only to their limited provincial outlook. Chaucer mocks indulgently, pretending to be impressed with them, but shows his valuation of this little cluster of slightly pompous figures by treating them not as individuals but collectively, as though they were all very much alike.

Medieval merchant or trade gilds were associations of men following the same craft or business. Their function was protective, giving their members exclusive trading rights within a town or area. The social gilds, to which these Five Gildsmen appear to belong, acted rather like mutual insurance societies, providing for their members a form of sickness benefit, a private chaplain and burial rites, and sometimes a school for their children. The pilgrimage gives Chaucer's gildsmen an opportunity of airing the distinctive costume or livery which each of the gilds adopted for ceremonial occasions.

365. *alle in o liveree* 'all dressed in the same livery', although they belong to five different trades. This suggests that the 'greet fraternitee' of line 366 is one of the social and religious gilds, like that of the Ludlow Palmers.

368. *chaped noght with bras* 'not encased in brass scabbards'. Chaucer ironically adopts the Gildsmen's sense of pride in their superior equipment.

371–2. 'each of them had the air of a dignified burgess seated on the raised platform of a gildhall', or meeting-place of the gild. This often was, or became, synonymous with a town hall. A burgess was a member of the governing body of a town or borough.

373. *for the wisdom that he kan* 'in respect of the knowledge and experience which he possessed.'

374. *shaply for to been* 'likely to be'.

375. *catel hadde they ynogh and rente* 'they had enough both of property (chattels) and of income to qualify as aldermen'.

376. *hir wives wolde it wel assente* 'their wives would certainly approve of their becoming aldermen', for the social prestige.

377. *were they to blame* 'they deserved to be censured'.
378. *to been ycleped 'madame'* In Chaucer's lifetime the social
rank of alderman was apparently the lowest which qualified a
wife for this form of address. It seems to have been coveted
by women with social pretensions, like the wife of the miller
in *The Reeve's Tale*, whom no one dared address in any other
fashion.
379. *goon to vigilies al bifore* 'to have precedence in the civic
procession to vigils', the religious services held on the eve of
a patronal saint's day. The Wife of Bath shares this feminine
love of precedence: see lines 451–2.
380. *a mantel roialliche ybore* To have one's cloak borne up like
a queen.

THE COOK. This is the shortest of the individual portraits,
supported by a fragmentary tale which breaks off after some
sixty lines. There is no personal description apart from the
mention of the ulcer on the Cook's leg which makes Chaucer
feel a little queasy, and a dry hint that he is a drunkard—a
weakness possibly encouraged by the heat of the kitchen. The
rest is an account of his accomplishment as chef, given with the
characteristic energy and assertiveness of Chaucer's mature
style, and completing the evidence of the poet's close familiarity
with one more aspect of medieval life, begun in the portrait of
the Franklin.

382. *to boille the chiknes with the marybones* One of the most
splendidly expressive lines in Chaucer, its rich variety of
consonants and vowel-sounds amplifying the description of an
appetising dish.
383. *poudre-marchant tart* A sharp-flavoured spice.
    galingale An aromatic root used as flavouring.
384. *wel koude he knowe* 'he was an expert judge of'; with a
suggestion that he drank a good deal. Later, the Cook is
found to be too drunk to tell his tale.
386. *mortreux* 'thick soup or stew'.
    a pie Meaning a pie containing meat. Fruit pies seem not
to have made their appearance until the sixteenth century.
387. *as it thoughte me* 'as it seemed to me'.
389. *blankmanger* Not the insipid blancmange known to us, but
a rich confection containing pounded chicken, rice, almonds,
eggs and cream.

Notes

THE SHIPMAN. Like most of his fellow-pilgrims, the Shipman is outstanding as a human being and as a member of his profession: a master-mariner of wide experience and ability, whose unrivalled knowledge of coasts and tides qualifies him for any undertaking by sea. The comment, 'With many a tempest hadde his berd been shake', gives us a glimpse of a medieval sea-dog from a county that, two centuries later, would produce the most daring and intrepid of English sailors. Like them, as Chaucer suggests by showing us the dagger hanging under his arm, the Shipman has an easy conscience towards piracy and theft, and no pity for his victims. He is the citizen of a tough, unsparing world outside the province of established law and order, where there can be no appeal to justice and where a man must depend upon himself; navigating without charts and defending his ship by his own force of arms. Ashore, awkwardly riding a horse as powerful as himself, the Shipman is temporarily less impressive; but Chaucer makes us recognize the force of his character: a man tanned and hardened by exposure, and deeply versed in the craft of the sea.

390. *woninge fer by weste* 'dwelling in the far west of England'.
391. *he was of Dertemouthe* 'he came from Dartmouth', in South Devon; a port notorious for its rough characters.
392. *as he kouthe* 'as best he knew'. Sailors are not usually good horsemen. His rouncy—a powerful carthorse—has features in common with the Shipman.
395. *under his arm adoun* 'hanging at his side beneath his arm'. Unlike the Yeoman, the Shipman does not openly display his weapon, though he keeps it ready for instant use.
399. *fro Burdeux-ward* 'during the voyage from Bordeaux', a port at the centre of the great wine-growing district of France.
   whil that the chapman sleep 'while the winemerchant was asleep'. Presumably he spent most of the voyage with his cargo.
400. *of nice conscience took he no keep* 'he wasn't troubled by tender feelings or regard for moral law': 'nice' meaning scrupulous.
401-2. If he fought with other ships and won the battle, he drowned his prisoners. The jocular expression suits the Shipman's unfeeling outlook: 'he sent them home by sea, wherever they came from'.

403. *of his crafte to rekene wel his tides* 'of his ability to predict the tides'. Modern seamen can look them up in a nautical almanac, but the Shipman had to be self-reliant.

404. *his stremes, and his daungers him bisides* 'the river-currents and the other hazards to navigation'. The possessive is here used to signify things which the Shipman has to deal with.

405. *his herberwe, and his moone, his lodemenage* 'his knowledge of harbours, of the moon [which causes tides and supposedly influences the weather] and of navigation'.

406. *Cartage* Cartagena in Spain.

407. *wys to undertake* 'reliable as master of an enterprise'.

409. *as they were* 'in successive order'.

410. *fro Gootlond to the cape of Finistere* 'from Gotland, an island off the coast of Sweden, to Finisterre in Brittany'. Alternatively, 'Gootlond' may mean Jutland.

411. *Britaigne* Bretagne or Brittany, a province on the north-west coast of France.

412. *his barge* Not of course a lighter, but a sea-going vessel with sails.

the Maudelaine The *Magdalene*; representing the medieval pronunciation still preserved in the colleges of that name at Oxford and at Cambridge. A Dartmouth vessel called the *Magdalene* paid customs duties in 1391, when her master was one Peter Risshenden. There are reasons for believing that Chaucer had this man in mind when he described the Shipman.

The Shipman, physically tough and coarsely dressed, is followed by a strangely contrasting figure. THE DOCTOR OF PHYSIC, in clothes lined with taffeta and sendal, is one of the most richly dressed of the pilgrims, and an outstanding member of a much respected profession. He is well-read in the Greek, Roman, Arab and more recent English medical authorities, and expert in diagnosing and treating sickness, both by drugs and by the use of natural magic, which required a considerable knowledge of astrology. It is only when Chaucer fills out the picture by supplying some details of the pilgrim's private character that he begins to reveal a similarity of outlook and way of life between the Physician and the piratical Shipman. One is openly lawless, robbing by physical violence and disposing of his victims with cold-blooded amusement; the other a more plausible thief, enriching himself under cover of professional ethics. Like the Shipman, the Physician has no feelings for others, and no regard for moral principle: 'his studie was but litel on the Bible', Chaucer remarks. Thanks partly to a secret agreement with his druggist, by which each increases the other's turnover, the Physician makes a good deal of money but hangs on to it like a miser, refusing to distribute alms. His principal object in life is not to bring health to his patients but to prolong his own existence by cautious habits and a moderate diet; and his consuming passion is gold. Under a veneer of respectability and wealth he passes for a learned and praiseworthy member of society, but his code of behaviour is based on avarice and self-regard, and unaffected by compassion.

415. *to speke of* 'in respect of'.
416. *grounded in astronomye* 'thoroughly instructed in astrology'. Before treating or operating upon his patient, a medieval doctor would take into consideration the aspects of the planets, in order to calculate the most favourable moment to begin his treatment.
417–18. The Physician kept close watch over his patient during the hours most auspicious for his recovery. There may be a suggestion in 'a ful greet deel' that the Physician assured his patient that the moment was favourable when in fact it was not, in order to obtain the fee for special treatment. Natural magic, as distinct from black magic or sorcery, made use of processes not understood in medieval times and now regarded as natural and not magic. The popular remedy of applying a piece of mouldy leather to a wound could appear magically effective through the presence of penicillin in the mould. The simply magical aspects of the Physician's practice might include treating a weapon instead of the wound it had made, or creating a wax image of his patient, under certain astrological conditions, in order to benefit his health. See Chaucer's *Hous of Fame*, III, 175 ff.
419. *wel koude he fortunen the ascendent* 'he was adept at engraving lucky charms with the astrological symbols most favourable to his patient'. The ascendant is the part of the zodiac just rising above the eastern horizon. (The subject is more fully explained in *An Introduction to Chaucer*, ch. 6.)
422. *hoot, or coold, or moist, or drie* The four conditions, two

of which are combined in each of the four elements of fire, air, water and earth, and also in the four humours or natural juices of the body—blood, choler, phlegm and black bile. An excess or lack of any one condition upset the balance of natural juices and produced a disease which the physician attempted to cure by restoring the balance of humours. (See *An Introduction to Chaucer*, ch. 6, for a more detailed explanation.)

424. *verray, parfit praktisour* 'truly perfect practitioner'.

425. *the cause yknowe, and of his harm the roote* 'having discovered the cause of the disease and the source of its ill-effects'.

429. *ech of hem made oother for to winne* 'each of them—the physician and the apothecary or druggist—provided the other with profitable business': the apothecary sending patients to the physician, and receiving prescriptions for drugs and medicines in return.

430. *nas nat newe to biginne* 'was of long standing'.

431–6. Of the eminent medical authorities cited here, the most famous are Aesculapius, the legendary god of medicine, 'olde Ypocras' or Hippocrates, of the fifth century B.C., and the Roman physician Galen who lived in the first century A.D. The last names in the list are those of thirteenth- and fourteenth-century authorities, two of them English and the third, Bernard Gordon, a Scot.

439. *of greet norissing and digestible* He ate sparingly, choosing what was most nutritious and easily digested. Evidently the Physician is more concerned to preserve his own health than to cure his patients.

440. *his studie was but litel on the Bible* The popular belief that doctors were atheists—encouraged probably by their study of Arab authors such as Avicenna, Hali and Averroes, who are included in the list above—persisted until the seventeenth century.

442. *lined with taffata and with sendal* Taffeta was a plain-woven glossy silk, sendal another form of silk material. Evidently the Physician spends lavishly upon his dress.

443. *esy of dispence* 'slow to spend money'.

444. *that he wan in pestilence* 'the fees he took during epidemics of plague'. By saying that he kept them, Chaucer implies that the Physician did not give away part of them as alms to relieve suffering.

445. *gold in phisik is a cordial* A medical preparation of gold called aurum potabile was prescribed as an infallible remedy. The fact invites the satirical remark of the next line.

THE WIFE OF BATH. Like all the great characters of literature, the Wife belongs to her own age without being limited to any historical epoch. In her brazen red stockings, her vast hat and wimple, she conforms with the standards of popular medieval life; noisy, assertive and robust. Her ruddy complexion, her deafness and her widely spaced teeth give her an emphatic personality such as few of the Pilgrims can rival. But the Wife also embodies certain timeless aspects of human character in general; in particular, the self-confident energy which has carried her through five marriages and three pilgrimages to the Holy Land. As the opening sentence of the *General Prologue* reveals, a pilgrimage was often an excuse for indulging a love of adventure and uninterrupted gossip, and it is hard to see her as devout. Her impulses are as overwhelmingly physical as the cushioning hips which seat her firmly upon her horse, or as the ten-pound coverchiefs which she wears on Sundays. She represents mankind's uninhibited enjoyment of its natural appetites, of raucous companionship, of adventurous curiosity and of pride in its exploits and achievements. She boasts no fastidious manners, has few social pretensions, and needs no more protection than the Shipman. A raw spirit of life bears her forward, jaunty and indestructible, like a cork on a stream.

Partly because it is so detailed, this is one of the most completely realized of the portraits. Chaucer describes the Wife's physical appearance and peculiarities, her conspicuous clothing and her mount, her emotional temper and her social manner. He outlines her matrimonial history and mentions some of the long pilgrimages which she has undertaken. But the portrait comes to life so vividly because all these points cohere, as parts of a single individuality. The fact that the Wife has 'thries been at Jerusalem' is not an isolated part of her personal record, but proof of the vitality and boundless self-confidence that are implicit in her scarlet stockings. The references to her hips, legs and spurs—none of which the Prioress appears to possess—and the admission that the Wife is 'gat-tothed', all emphasize the physical nature of a woman whose clamorous impulses have driven her five times to the church door. We do not need the evidence of the Wife's prologue, where for eight hundred and fifty lines she talks about herself almost without drawing breath, to realize that Chaucer was fascinated by her. This introductory portrait, as sharp-edged and brilliant as a manuscript illumination, shows how closely his imagination was held by a figure whose vitality and appetite for experience rivalled his own.

447. *a good Wif* 'a goodwife', the mistress of a house or other establishment.

448. *somdel deef* 'somewhat deaf': the result of a domestic battle recounted in her prologue, lines 788–96, when her fifth husband strikes her after she has torn three pages out of his book against women.

449. *swich an haunt* 'such skill'.

450. *Ypres and . . . Gaunt* Or Ghent, rich and important Flemish cloth-weaving cities from which many weavers emigrated to England during the fourteenth century.

451. *wif ne was ther noon* 'there was no woman whatever'; 'wife' being a term for a mature woman of the poorer classes, not necessarily married.

452. *bifore hire sholde goon* 'who was permitted to make her offering before the Wife'. The congregation went up to the altar-steps in order of social precedence. Cf. line 379.

454. *out of alle charitee* 'enraged'; with word-play on the charitable purpose of the offering. People out of charity with others were supposed not to make an offering: see Matt. v. 23, 24.

455. *coverchiefs* Cloths used as covering for the head or neck, *chief* being Old French for head. They were arranged on elaborate wire structures, which gave the head a grotesquely distorted shape.

ful fine weren of ground 'were of finest texture'.

459. *ful streite yteyd* 'stretched tightly over the leg'.

462. *housbondes at chirche dore* Until the sixteenth century, the wedding ceremony took place at the door of the church, and was followed by nuptial mass at the altar.

463. *withouten* 'not to speak of'.

464. *therof nedeth nat to speke as nowthe* 'we don't have to talk about that at this moment'. Perhaps Chaucer was planning to say more about the Wife's youthful indiscretions at some later stage, or had already written the prologue to her tale, where she herself describes her gay life as a young woman. His

remark draws attention to her sins under the pretext of trying to dismiss the subject, as though saying, 'I'm sure we don't want to hear about that'.

466. *passed many a straunge strem* 'crossed many foreign rivers'.

467–8. *Rome, Boloigne, Galice, Coloigne* Four of the most famous centres of pilgrimage: the Holy City, Boulogne, St James of Compostella in Galicia, and Cologne.

469. *she koude muchel* 'she knew much'.

wandringe by the weye seems deliberately ambiguous, with a covert allusion to the Wife's moral swervings—perhaps on a pilgrimage.

470. *gat-tothed* 'with widely spaced teeth'. In her prologue the Wife asserts that this feature 'bicam me weel'—suited her. It was taken to be a sign of wantonness.

471. *upon an amblere* 'on an ambling horse', allowing her to ride along in untroubled comfort.

esily she sat, since it came naturally to her to dominate calmly: but she chooses a docile victim.

472. *ywimpled wel* 'her wimple gracefully arranged', or—perhaps more probably—wearing a fine wimple (a garment wrapped about the head and neck to frame the face).

473. *a bokeler or a targe* The comparison with pieces of military equipment helps to suggest the Wife's boldly aggressive character. Like the spurs mentioned later, they denote her love of dominating the male.

474. *a foot-mantel* An outer garment worn to protect the dress. The Wife rode astride like a man. The feminine custom of riding side-saddle was introduced into England by Anne of Bohemia, Richard II's first queen, but was evidently not adopted outside the court.

475. *a paire of spores sharpe* Another pointed indication of the Wife's domineering character, and readiness to tyrannize.

476. *carpe* 'talk, chatter'; without the sense of cavilling or criticizing which the term has since acquired. The Wife comes naturally to the fore as a gossip, not attempting to imitate the ladylike coyness of the Prioress.

477. *per chaunce* 'it is possible'.

remedies of love Probably meaning love-potions or aphrodisiacs rather than ways of mending a broken heart.

478. *she koude of that art the olde daunce* 'she knew all the ins and outs of that game'.

THE PARSON. This is the second longest of the portraits, and the most serious. The Parson is an embodiment of strenuous moral virtue in a world corrupted by avarice and self-seeking; the one ecclesiastical figure among the Pilgrims who has not betrayed his Master for the sake of material profit or the good estimation of his fellows. He represents the trustful, patient faith that holds firm while standards are collapsing on all sides and weaker men in higher places are—in their own eyes— coming to terms with the realities of a dissolute age. Here, at the centre of the *General Prologue*, for fifty lines Chaucer's irony is silent as he reveals his respect for the integrity of the good shepherd of a country parish, who tends his human flock while more ambitious priests desert their congregations for a more agreeable way of life in London. There is no physical description, no reference to the Parson's individual habits or to his private history; yet a strong sense of personality emerges from this detailed account of fidelity to a religious calling. If the portrait has any satirical purpose, it must work outwards from the Parson; showing that the sense of mission crushed by the accumulated wealth of the Church survives where it is least regarded, among the country clergy who devote their lives to the care of their humble and ignorant parishioners.

480. *persoun of a toun* 'priest of a hamlet or country parish': see line 493.
482. *a clerk* A learned man like the Clerk of Oxenford, though now living actively for the good of others.
487. *ypreved ofte sithes* 'proved many times'.
488. *to cursen for his tithes* A parishioner who did not pay his annual tithe—a tenth part of his income—to the priest might be excommunicated. The Parson was unwilling to call for such punishment. 'Rather wolde he yeven'; in marked contrast to the close-fisted Physician.
489. *out of doute* 'it is certain'.
491. *offring, substaunce.* The Easter offering is presented to the priest. The Parson uses this, and also his own possessions, to relieve the needs of his parishioners.
492. *he koude in litel thing have suffisaunce* 'he knew how to be content with a modest sufficiency'.
493. *wyd was his parisshe* 'his parish was extensive'.
495. *in meschief* 'those in trouble or misfortune'.
496. *muche and lite* 'rich and poor alike'.

497. *upon his feet, and in his hand a staf* The image specifically associates the Parson with Christ's apostles, who travelled in the same fashion to spread the gospel. The Parson evidently cannot afford a horse, and does his pastoral work the hard way.

498. *his sheep* 'his parishioners', with allusion to the figure of Christ the good shepherd.

499. *first he wroghte* 'first he did charitable deeds', giving himself the right to preach Christ's doctrine to others.

500. *out of the gospel* Matt. v. 19: 'Whoso shall do and teach them [the commandments of Christ], the same shall be called great in the kingdom of heaven.'

501. *this figure* 'figure of speech', proverbial saying.

502. *If gold ruste, what shal iren do?* If the priest cannot resist temptation, how should his flock do better?

504. *no wonder is a lewed man to ruste* 'it isn't surprising if a layman, usually an unlearned person, becomes morally corrupt'.

505. *take keep* 'take note'.

509. *he sette nat his benefice to hire* He didn't leave his parish in charge of a curate, paying him part of the stipend which he continued to draw as priest.

512. *to seken him a chaunterie for soules* To try to obtain a chantry at St Paul's, where he would be paid to sing daily masses for the repose of a rich man's soul.

513. *or with a bretherhed to been withholde* 'or to be retained as chaplain to a fraternity or gild'.

514. *kepte wel his folde* 'watched over his flock, his parish, conscientiously'.

515. *ne made it nat miscarie* 'did not bring it to harm': the double negative being used as a more emphatic form of negative construction, as at lines 430, 451, 494 and *passim*.

516. *noght a mercenarie* 'not a hireling'. The reference is to John x.12: 'He that is an hireling, and not the shepherd, whose own the sheep are not, seeth the wolf coming, and leaveth the sheep, and fleeth.'

519. *ne...daungerous ne digne* 'neither arrogant nor haughty'.

521. *by fairnesse* 'by gentle means'.

523. *but it were* 'unless it were'.

525. *for the nonis* 'immediately'.

527. *he waited after* 'he expected'.

528. *a spiced conscience* 'a dainty or over-scrupulous sense of

moral duty'. Spices are added to things which have gone bad, to disguise the corruption. The phrase recurs in *The Wife of Bath's Prologue*, line 435.

529. *Cristes loore and his apostles twelve* 'the teaching of Christ and of the apostles'.

THE PLOWMAN. As we see from Chaucer's fabliaux, characters from the lower classes of society were usually brought into medieval literature to provide grotesque and farcical figures. But Chaucer's presentation of the Plowman is entirely respectful. Like the hero of Langland's religious poem, *Piers Plowman*, this pilgrim is an honest worker, a small tenant farmer serving God through his uncomplaining work and by his charity towards his fellow-men, paying his debts and living in peace with his neighbours. Without disguising the lowly nature of his work, Chaucer allows the Plowman the simple dignity of an ancient and essential occupation and the strength of the creed which he honours through his daily life. He is respected as one of the small number of pilgrims whose motives in undertaking this springtime excursion are above suspicion.

531. *plowman* Used generically of workers on the land.

532. *that hadde ylad of dong ful many a fother* 'who had carried many a cartload of manure'; doing the 'dirty work' of enriching the soil for the general good of society. Despite his lowliness, the plowman is an indispensable figure of the social system.

536. *thogh him gamed or smerte* 'whether in pleasure or in pain'; in all circumstances.

537. *and thanne his neighebor right as himselve* 'next after loving God he loved his fellow-men as himself'; see Matt. xxii. 37–9.

538. *therto dike and delve* 'also make ditches and dig'.

540. *withouten hire* 'without asking payment'; again in marked contrast to the professional classes.

542. *his propre swink and his catel* He paid his tithes partly by working on the priest's land and partly in kind, by the produce of his own holding.

543. *a mere* 'a mare'; a humble mount, probably his own cart-horse.

544–6. This preliminary list of six pilgrims, five of whom are then described in detail, has the appearance of a summary which Chaucer expanded later. It serves to remind the reader how far the cataloguing of the company has progressed, and shows that the list is nearly complete.

546. *and myself* Modesty prevents Chaucer from offering any account of his own life-history and personal appearance. As the observer of the other pilgrims rather than a fully integrated member of their company he keeps in the background of the *General Prologue*. As noticed above in the Introduction, he brings himself shyly into the picture later, when the Host calls him forward. He also includes a reference to himself as an over-prolific writer by making the Man of Law complain that 'thogh he kan but lewedly on metres', Chaucer has already told every story, in one book or another. (*Introduction to the Man of Law's Tale*, lines 46–52.)

THE MILLER. Here Chaucer returns to farcical realism and the grotesque figures of a world remote from the moral ideal represented by the Parson and the Plowman. The Miller is more of an animal than of a human being: powerfully muscular, frighteningly ugly, sly, coarse and brutally insensitive. His huge black nostrils and gaping mouth suggest the distorted expression of a gargoyle, and the din he creates with his bagpipe and his raucous conversation associate him with the howling demons of a medieval Last Judgement. Chaucer may have had this comparison in mind when he gave the Miller a mouth like 'a greet forneys'. It is a brief but completely integrated portrait; features, physique, habits and dress all combining to embody human beastliness, with a dangerous violence of temper lurking beneath the surface of the man's rowdy good-fellowship. This is the nature which breaks out when the Knight cómes to the end of his tale and the Miller insists, with drunken oaths, upon telling his tale next in contempt of precedence.

547. *a stout carl* 'a powerfully-built churl' or low-class person.

for the nones 'extremely'.

548. *ful big he was of brawn* 'with great muscles'.

549. *over al ther he cam* 'wherever he went'. Chaucer may have intended a grotesque parallel with the prowess of the Knight, who always won 'a sovereyn prys'.

550. *the ram* The champion's prize. In Switzerland, where wrestling is still a national sport, the champion is awarded a young bull.

Notes

551. *a thikke knarre* 'a sturdy tough'.

552. *heve of harre* 'lift off its hinges'; perhaps with a suggestion of antisocial violence, as of a burglar breaking into a house.

557. *a werte* This wart, with its tuft of sow's-bristles, epitomizes the ugly brutishness of the Miller's nature.

561. In medieval pictures and sculpture, hell is shown as just such a gaping mouth.

562. *a janglere and a goliardeys* 'a noisy gossip and coarse buffoon'.

563. *moost of sinne and harlotries* 'his usual conversation was scurrilous and obscene'. His taste for indecency is displayed in *The Miller's Tale*.

564. *tollen thries* The Miller took payment in kind for grinding corn by deducting a proportion of the customer's flour, but he stole twice as much again. As everyone who grew a little corn for sale or use had to take it to be milled, it was difficult to escape this form of extortion. The miller described in *The Reeve's Tale* is another dishonest one: 'A theef he was for sothe of corn and mele'.

565. *a thombe of gold* Evidently a proverbial reference to the dishonesty of millers. His thumb acquired a distinctive shape through feeling samples of corn. Through his skill and dishonesty, this thumb brought him wealth.

566. *a whit cote* Which would not show flour dust.

567. *a baggepipe* An instrument which medieval pictures often show in the mouths of devils.

THE MANCIPLE. The duties of a manciple were to purchase food supplies and provisions for an institution such as a college, a monastery or one of the Inns of Court, whose inmates lived as a society and ate communal meals. As this usually called for large purchases, there was room for making handsome profits by sly or long-sighted business deals; and here Chaucer's Manciple excels. Apart from praising the shrewdness which he considers, or pretends to consider, remarkable in a man of no formal education, Chaucer does not say much about the man. Ten of the twenty lines are given over to a mocking comparison between the 'expert and curious masters' and the illiterate servant who surpasses them in business acumen—and, apparently, in sharp practices. Rather than describing the Manciple, Chaucer seems to be continuing the satire of the legal

Notes

profession begun in the portrait of the Man of Law. The term
'gentil', applied ironically, is the only possible allusion to the
Manciple's personal qualities. His dress and appearance are not
described, and he remains physically a shadowy figure.

569. *of a temple* Employed either in the Middle Temple or the
Inner Temple, two of the Inns of Court in London which
provided living quarters for lawyers.

570. *take exemple* 'learn something'. The remark is ironic,
because the Manciple was dishonest. But the lawyers are
expected to be dishonest too, so the irony is compounded.

571. *wise* By extension, 'wise' comes to mean astute, and
crooked.

572. *paide or took by taille* Literally, paid cash or bought on
credit; 'taille' being the tally or notched stick on which
purchases were recorded. But 'took' hints again at the
Manciple's cheating.

573. *he waited so in his achaat* He bided his time, buying when
prices were most advantageous.

574. *he was ay biforn and in good staat* 'he always had something
in hand and was financially sound'; probably with something
in his own pocket.

575. *of God a ful fair grace* 'a gracious gift of God'. The
question seems innocent, but is full of irony. The 'wit' of the
Manciple which surpasses the 'wisdom' of the lawyers means
the wily dishonesty at which he was even more adept than
these foxy professional men. Chaucer asks whether it isn't
remarkable that a simple man should be so talented.

576. *a lewed mannes wit* 'an uneducated man's intelligence'.

578. *maistres* 'doctors of law'.

579. *expert and curious* 'skilled and meticulous'.

581. *stiwardes of rente and lond* The steward or seneschal of a
great estate controlled its domestic affairs, regulated expendi-
ture and appointed officers and servants.

583. *by his propre good* 'on his own income'. The reference is
to the lord.

584. *in honour dettelees* 'without dishonourable debts'.
but if he were wood 'unless he were out of his mind'.

585. *scarsly as him list desire* 'as economically as he wished';
literally, 'as it pleased him to wish'.

586. *able for to helpen al a shire* 'able to help anyone'; literally,
all the inhabitants of a county.

587. *in any caas that mighte falle or happe* 'in any eventuality that might occur'.

588. *sette hir aller cappe* 'made fools of them all', by his quicker wit.

THE REEVE. The normal duties of a reeve were to superintend a landowner's estates and tenants. This particular Reeve seems to have combined some of the functions of steward and bailiff with his own proper duties: compare line 595 and lines 600–1. Chaucer's deeply perceptive character-study could be read simply as the description of a medieval type—the choleric man, physically lean and dry, crafty, ambitious and revengeful in temper, watchfully alert. But Chaucer's analysis of the Reeve takes him far beyond the limitations of medieval physiology. He sees, in the man's bony legs, his cropped hair and his habit of shaving 'as ny as ever he kan', the manifestation of a mean, uncharitable nature which makes the Reeve's subordinates go in dread of his malice. His aim in life is to get the better of everyone, and he ridicules the attempts of auditors to catch him out in the embezzling by which he has quietly enriched himself. By dwelling on the heath outside the town he shows his hatred of humanity, isolating himself like a wolf who rejects all companionship, and ingratiating himself only with those who have goods to steal. His chosen place at the back of the other pilgrims reveals a man too mistrustful of his fellow-men to expose himself. He expects of them the same contempt for human feelings, the same unscrupulous regard for private advantage, as dominate his own warped and spiteful existence.

589. *a sclendre colerik man* A man in whom the humour of choler predominated, giving him a testy and irascible nature and a body fretted by its own heat into wiry thinness. (See *An Introduction to Chaucer*, ch. 6, for further details.)

592. *dokked lyk a preest biforn* His hair was clipped short in front, like a priest who has taken the tonsure. Among the laity, close-cropped hair was a mark of servile status. It had its practical use in allowing lice to be caught more easily. Long hair presupposed the habit of washing or at least combing.

595. *kepe a gerner and a binne* 'keep good watch over the granary and the corn-bin'.

596. *noon auditour koude on him winne* 'no auditor could catch him out in his accounts'.

597–8. He could closely estimate, from the rainfall and the extent of the dry spells, what crops and what harvest could be expected.

601. *hoolly in this Reves governinge* 'managed completely by the Reeve'.

602. *by his covenant yaf the rekeninge* by the terms of his contract, the Reeve rendered the accounts—normally the duty of the steward.

604. *bringe him in arrerage* 'accuse him of not paying bills when they were due'.

606. *that he ne knew his sleighte and his covine* 'whose deceitful tricks he was not familiar with', and perhaps used himself.

607. *the deeth* Either the plague—the Black Death—or death itself.

610. *he koude bettre than his lord purchace* 'he knew how to get possession of property more adroitly, or at a better price, than his master'.

611. *astored prively* 'putting money and goods away secretly'. From this point of view it would be convenient to live apart, in a house screened by trees.

613. *to yeve and lene him of his owene good* 'making him gifts and loans out of his master's own property' which the Reeve had appropriated.

614. *and yet a cote and hood* 'with a rent-free cottage (cote) and a coat (hood) into the bargain'; the perquisites of the Reeve's office.

615. *myster* 'a mystery, or profession'; see next line.

616. *a wel good wrighte* 'a skilful craftsman'.

619. *surcote of pers* 'a grey-blue outer coat'.

620. *a rusty blade* As noted in the Introduction, the only piece of personal equipment mentioned in the *General Prologue* which is not sharp, bright and polished: compare lines 114, 359–60, 367.

622. *Baldeswelle* Bawdeswell in Norfolk, about fifteen miles north-west of Norwich. Bawdeswell Heath (line 608) lies south-west of the town. Chaucer was named as surety for Sir William de Beauchamp when, in 1378, he was granted the custody of property and estates which included Bawdeswell. Sir William's management of the estate was the subject of an official investigation in 1386–7, by which date Chaucer either had begun, or was about to begin work on the *Canterbury Tales*. The character of the Reeve may owe something to this connexion.

623. *tukked...as is a frere* His long surcoat tucked into his girdle, like a friar's habit.

624. *the hindreste of oure route* 'the last man of the company, behind the rest'.

THE SUMMONER. During the Middle Ages, the clergy were exempt from the powers of the civil courts, and for all offences except treason were tried by ecclesiastic courts. As we see from *The Friar's Tale* [Robinson III. 1586–1621,] these courts were also empowered to try laymen for moral offences such as adultery, and to punish by fines or excommunication. Wrongdoers were ordered to attend the courts by summoners, who seem also to have acted as informers to the authority they served.

Chaucer's Summoner, described approvingly as 'a gentil harlot' and 'a bettre felawe', is a gross and disreputable creature who shares and encourages the faults of the offenders whom he summons to court. Like the Miller, he is betrayed by his face. The marks of a revolting disease which nothing will remove, the scabs and white blotches in his burning red cheeks, the narrow eyes and dropping hair which make him a terror to children, complement a loathsome moral nature. His taste for highly flavoured food and strong wine reveals his coarse appetite, and his drunken shouting and babbling suggest how far animal impulses dominate him. As an officer he is venal and easily corruptible, taking bribes to conceal offences and speaking contemptuously of the archdeacon who presides over the court. His disgusting habits and appearance represent the moral standards of the judicial system which employs him.

626. *cherubinnes* cherubim, once spelt cherubin, is the plural form of cherub. In early Christian art cherubim were evidently coloured red. This association of the Summoner with a celestial being is deeply ironic.

627. *saucefleem* Disfigured by a form of leprosy called *salsum-flegma*, supposedly aggravated by pungent foods; see line 636.

629. *scalled browes blake and piled berd* 'scabby black eyebrows and a beard with hairs dropping out'. Characteristically, Chaucer gives disease and a revolting appearance to a man whom he recognizes as unredeemably evil.

632. *ne oille of tartre noon* 'nor yet any oil of tartar', a saturated solution of potassium carbonate.

634. *that him mighte helpen* 'that might cure him': compare line 18, 'That hem hath holpen'.

643. *he herde it al the day* In the ecclesiastical court to which he summoned delinquents.

645. *Watte* 'Walter', as a parrot says 'Poll'.

646. *whoso koude in oother thing him grope* 'if anyone tested his knowledge further'.

648. *Questio quid iuris* 'the question is, which part of the law?'.

649. *a gentil harlot* Superficially, a term of energetic approval, as we might call a friend a rogue; 'gentil' having the sense of well-bred, courteous, gentlemanly, and 'harlot' meaning a villain. But Chaucer's respect is ironic, as when he describes the Manciple as 'gentil'. In both pilgrims 'gentilesse', whether social or moral, is conspicuously absent.

651–3. For the price of a drink, he would agree to keep quiet for a year about a man's mistress-keeping, and make nothing of his offence. It was just such sins that the ecclesiastical courts were intended to deal with.

654. *ful prively a finch eek koude he pulle* 'he also knew how to pluck a finch in secret'; probably meaning that the Summoner swindled or fleeced unsuspecting victims.

655. *a good felawe* 'an accomplice'; probably another rascally Summoner, who joined him in a confidence trick.

656–7. *to have noon awe in swich caas of the ercedekenes curs* 'not to be afraid of being excommunicated for such offences'. The archdeacon, as representative of the bishop, pronounced the sentence.

658. *but if a mannes soule were in his purs* 'unless, of course, a man kept his soul in his purse': then he would be in danger of losing it to the archdeacon.

659. *in his purs he sholde ypunisshed be* Meaning that the offender could buy himself off by paying a heavy fine; a satirical reference to the venality of the ecclesiastical courts.

660. *purs is the ercedekenes helle* An offender is made to suffer financially, not to endure hell-fire. In this way the Church profited from sin.

661. *he lied right in dede* 'he told a downright lie'.

662. *him drede* 'to go in fear' (of excommunication).

663. *curs wol slee right as assoilling savith* 'excommunication will damn a sinner just as surely as absolution will save his soul'.

664. *and also war him of a 'Significavit'* 'and also be careful to avoid imprisonment by the ecclesiastical court'. 'Significavit nobis venerabilis pater' were the opening words of a writ committing an excommunicated person to prison.

665. *in daunger hadde he at his owene gise* 'he had complete personal control of'.
666. *yonge girles* Young people of both sexes.
668. *al hir reed* 'adviser to them all'.
669. *an ale-stake* A pole set up in front of an alehouse, bearing a garland or bush as a trade sign.
670. *a bokeleer hadde he maad him of a cake* 'he had made himself a shield out of a flat loaf of bread'. Taken with the 'gerland' or chaplet of the previous couplet, this huge loaf suggests a carnival mood, or the clownishness of a man determined to prove himself a genial companion—'a good felawe' —despite his sinister calling. Both chaplet and loaf are incongruously at odds with this serious official function, and with the Summoner's personal hideousness. Like the Pardoner who is his close friend, he seems to be trying to distract attention from the warning signs of his evil nature by assuming a cheerfulness of manner, or 'jolitee'. Instead, he draws attention to the imposture by the very flamboyance of his assumed gaiety. At the same time, the Summoner shows how little respect he feels for his function as an officer of justice, and, conversely, how little he himself deserves to be respected.

The Summoner and THE PARDONER form a pair, as close companions in what seems to be a homosexual attachment. They make their appearance singing together a love-song which is even more inappropriate to the Pardoner's calling than to the Summoner's. They are also partners in a deeply religious sense. Summoning, as the medieval play of *The Summoning of Everyman* reminds us, is a prelude not only to a session of the ecclesiastic courts but to divine judgement; and pardoning follows as a consequence of divine grace. But these two representatives of the most profound part of man's spiritual life are both diseased and blind to their own moral significance, intent instead upon being accepted as gaily irresponsible men of the world. Beneath the strained semblance of amiability lies spiritual rottenness.

Like all but a few of the nine-and-twenty, the last of the pilgrims is ruled by avarice. He has two sources of income: the holy relics for which he claims miraculous powers, and which the faithful may touch for a small charge, and plenary indulgences—the 'pardoun' crammed into his wallet. The purchaser of such a document did not in fact obtain pardon for a particular sin, but a spiritual allowance which might be set against his misdeeds, as though he were building up a credit balance against spiritual debts. During the fourteenth century the growing practice of selling indulgences enriched the Church, but aroused much moral indignation; and in the next century Luther's open attack upon the abuse was a move which led to the Reformation. Chaucer's account of the Pardoner reflects the popular feeling against a hypocritical profession. The full extent of his spiritual emptiness appears in the prologue to his tale, where the Pardoner boasts of his fraudulence and cheating under the guise of religion. The description of his character in the *General Prologue* prepares us for the damning disclosures to come.

Physically, the Pardoner is the victim of a cruel practical joke on the part of nature, which by not bringing him to sexual maturity has effectively neutered him. Chaucer's contemptuous remark, 'I trowe he were a gelding or a mare', should not be taken as insensitive, since he has given the Pardoner this humiliating defect in order to emphasize his spiritual sterility. With his piping voice and boyish complexion goes a feature which typifies the Pardoner's lack of manly vitality—the long but meagre and colourless locks falling to his shoulders, like strands of hair on a mummified corpse. To offset this macabre appearance, the Pardoner tries to pass himself off as a gay young man, affecting a fashionable negligence of dress, and singing love-songs with the repulsive Summoner. But this incongruous behaviour, like the jerky movements of a puppet, merely draws attention to its own artificiality. This creature whose inner life has shrivelled up is an uncreative dummy living as a parasite upon a religion to which he feels no sense of duty, exploiting the simple faith of his congregation for his private profit, and relishing the taste of his cynical triumph.

672. *of Rouncivale* From the hospital—in our sense, hostel—of St Mary Roncevall, near Charing Cross in London.

673. *the court of Rome* The Vatican, the source of papal indulgences. The Pardoner gives himself importance by this doubtful claim.

675. *bar to him a stif burdoun* 'accompanied him by singing the ground melody in a powerful voice'. The remark has unpleasant overtones.

678. *a strike of flex* 'a hank of flax', suggesting a dry and

unkempt bundle of dead hair. Note that he is not 'dokked lyk a preest', as the Reeve is.

679. *by ounces* Colloquially 'in rats' tails'.

681. *by colpons oon and oon* 'in strands here and there'.

682. *for jolitee* 'to cut a dashing figure'.

683. *trussed up in his walet* 'packed in his saddlebag'.

684. *al of the newe jet* 'in quite the latest style'.

685. *dischevelee, save his cappe, he rood al bare* 'he rode bare-headed except for a skull-cap, with disordered hair'.

686. *glaringe eyen* 'bulging eyes'.

689. *pardoun* 'indulgences', explained in the introductory paragraph above.

691. *ne nevere sholde have* The Pardoner can never acquire the normal sexual attributes of a man.

692. *late shave* 'freshly shaved'.

693. *a gelding or a mare* 'a eunuch or a woman'. The Pardoner's want of masculine characteristics is rudely alluded to by the Host at the end of *The Pardoner's Tale*, lines 952–5.

694. *fro Berwik into Ware* 'from Berwick-on-Tweed to Ware, in Hertfordshire'; from one end of the country to the other.

696. *in his male* 'in his baggage'.

700. *til Jhesu Crist him hente* 'until he was called to be a disciple': see Matt. iv. 18–20. Previously Peter had been a fisherman.

701. *crois of latoun* 'cheap metal cross'. Latten is a compound of zinc and copper.

702. *pigges bones* which he was passing off as holy relics.

704. *upon lond* 'somewhere'.

706. *than that the person gat* 'than the parson earned'.

707. *feyned flaterie and japes* 'insincere flattery and fraudulence'.

708. 'he made fools of parson and congregation together'.

712. *alderbest* 'best of all'.

714. *he moste preche* 'he would be expected to preach'.
     and wel affile his tonge 'and make a smoothly persuasive address'.

717. *in a clause* 'briefly'.

718. *th'estaat, th'array* 'their social status and dress'.

721. *faste by the Belle* Close to the Bell, a house of which nothing is certainly known.

723. *how that we baren us that ilke night* 'how we conducted ourselves that same evening'—in short, what we did.

724. *alight* 'dismounted, broke our journey'.

727. *of youre curteisye* 'by your indulgence'.

728. *n'arette it nat my vileynie* 'don't put it down to my bad taste or boorishness'.

730. *hir wordes and hir cheere* The words and facial expressions which they used.

731. *ne thogh I speke hir wordes proprely* Literally, 'even if I repeat their words exactly'; with the implication that Chaucer will show them up through their own words, 'proprely' then meaning appropriately.

734. *he moot reherce* 'he must repeat'.

735. *everich a word, if it be in his charge* 'every word, if it lies in his power'.

736. *al speke he* 'although he then speak'.
   rudeliche and large 'using vulgar and broad language'. Chaucer repeats this self-defensive caution before embarking on *The Miller's Tale*.

738. *or feyne thing* 'or invent something innocuous'.

739. *he may nat spare* 'he can't compromise, or withhold the truth'.
   althogh he were his brother Even though the story-teller were the poet's brother.

740. *he moot as wel seye o word as another* He must repeat the indecent words as well as the decent ones.

743. *eek Plato seith* Chaucer repeats the observation in *The Manciple's Tale*, lines 208-10:

> The word moot nede accorde with the dede,
> If men shal telle proprely a thing,
> The word moot cosin be to the werking.

746. *al have I nat* 'if I have not'.
   in hir degree 'in order of social rank'.

748. *my wit is short* throughout his work Chaucer describes himself as ineffectual and impractical, knowing—as here— that his readers will see through the comic pretence.

749. *greet chiere* 'an effusive welcome'.

750. *to the soper sette he us* 'he made us sit down to supper'.

751. *vitaille at the beste* 'excellent food'.

752. *wel to drinke us leste* 'we were very pleased to drink'.

THE HOST. Of all the pilgrims, Harry Bailly—named in the prologue to *The Cook's Tale*—is most likely to have been drawn from life. An innkeeper of that name lived in Southwark during the latter part of the fourteenth century. He was evidently a man of some consequence, representing Southwark as member of Parliament between 1376 and 1379, and acting as tax-collector and coroner over the period 1377–94. There is a record of his carrying money from the Custom House to the Treasurer of the Household in 1384, when Chaucer was Controller of Customs. If Harry Bailly knew Chaucer in his capacity of civil servant, there is an added joke in the Host's mockery of the poet as a timidly unobtrusive person of no importance. As a character of the *Tales*, the Host has several features in common with another pilgrim—the Monk. Both are genial, expansive, pleasure-loving men of the world with authority of character, and both have 'eyen stepe' and a robust physique. We learn later, however, that the Host goes in terror of his aggressive wife Godelief, and it seems that in proposing to accompany the pilgrims as judge of their stories the Host may be seeking a short respite from the trials of domestic life. If he is incapable of containing Godelief's outbursts of rage, the Host proves himself none the less to be a masterful yet considerate organizer of the very mixed party of pilgrims, using his authority wisely and humanely to hold them together during the various crises that arise, and infusing the whole pilgrimage with his own good-natured generosity.

754. *marchal in an halle* 'master of ceremonies in a great house'.

755. *with eyen stepe* 'with large, prominent eyes', like the Monk (line 201).

756. *burgeys* 'burgess'; a freeman of a borough.

Chepe 'Cheapside'; one of the main streets of medieval London, running from St Paul's to the bottom of Cornhill.

757. *boold of his speche* Not meaning that he was rudely out-spoken, but authoritative and commanding. He needs this quality during the pilgrimage, to repress arguments and out-breaks of dissension among the pilgrims, and also to put an end to boring stories. For an example of the Host's courtesy and tactfulness, see the Introduction, p. 23.

wel ytaught Not well educated, but well informed. The Host shows little respect towards formal education.

758. *of manhod him lakkede right naught* 'none of the attributes a man should possess was lacking in him': a marked contrast with the Pardoner.

760. *pleyen he bigan* 'began to exchange pleasantries and chaff'.

Notes

762. *maad oure rekeninges* 'settled our bills'. Evidently the pilgrims paid for their lodging in advance.

763. *lordinges* A polite form of address equivalent to 'sirs'.

767. *atones in this herberwe* 'all at the same time in this inn'.

768. *fain wolde I doon yow mirthe* 'I should like very much to provide entertainment for you'.

770. *to doon yow ese* 'to give you pleasure'.

771. *God yow speede* 'may God prosper your journey'.

772. *quite yow youre meede* 'reward you as you deserve'.

774. *ye shapen yow to talen* 'you intend to tell stories'.

775. *confort ne mirthe is noon* 'it's no pleasure'.

780. *for to stonden at my juggement* 'to abide by my decision'.

784. *but ye be mirie* 'if you don't enjoy yourselves'.

787. *to make it wys* 'to deliberate, to defer our answer'.

789. *seye his voirdit* 'tell us his proposal'.

790. *herkneth for the beste* 'listen carefully'. The Host is using the polite imperative form.

793. *to shorte with oure weye* 'to pass away the time during the journey'.

794–6. As noted above in the Introduction, the Host's proposal means that every pilgrim would tell four tales, amounting to a hundred and twenty tales in all. Chaucer later found this undertaking too ambitious, and reduced it considerably by making the Host expect only one tale from each pilgrim. Even this project was left incomplete, though before *The Parson's Tale* the Host declares that it needs only this final story to fulfil his condition. This anomaly, and the unchanged original proposal in the *General Prologue*, characterize the unfinished state of the *Canterbury Tales*.

800. *of best sentence and moost solaas* 'the most instructive and enjoyable'. The result of the competition is never declared, but on this basis of judgement the Nun's Priest would be a strong contender for the prize.

801. *at oure aller cost* 'at the expense of the rest of us'.

805. *goodly with yow ride* 'accompany you as a considerate friend'.

806. *right at myn owene cost* 'with no charge for my services'.

807. *whoso wole my juggement withseye* 'anyone who contests my authority as arbiter'.

809. *if ye vouche sauf* 'if you graciously allow this'.

811. *I wol erly shape me therfore* 'I will prepare myself for this at break of day'.

813. *and preyden him also* 'and furthermore we begged him'.
817. *sette a soper at a certeyn prys* 'arrange a supper at a stipu-
lated price'.
818. *at his devys* 'as he planned it'.
819. *in heigh and lough* 'in all respects'.
820. *we been acorded* 'we consented with'.
821. *the wyn was fet anon* Taking a drink together seals the
agreement.
825. *was oure aller cok* 'roused us all'.
827. *a litel moore than paas* 'at hardly more than walking pace'.
828. *the wateringe of Seint Thomas* St Thomas a Waterings, a
point two miles outside London on the Canterbury road,
where horses were watered.
829. *bigan his hors areste* 'drew up his horse': compare note on
line 303 above.
831. *I it yow recorde* 'I recall it to your minds'.
832. *if even-song and morwe-song accorde* 'if you are ready to
stand by last night's promise'.
834. *as evere mote I drinke* 'so may I ever drink'; an expression
roughly equivalent to the modern 'so help me'.
837. *draweth cut* A simple form of lottery in which straws of
different length are drawn, the uneven one deciding the issue.
This form of lottery is used by the rioters in *The Pardoner's
Tale*, lines 793–6.
    er that we ferrer twinne 'before we go any further'. The
literal sense of 'twinne' is to separate or set out, in this case
from London.
840. *draweth* Like 'cometh' and 'studieth' below, another
example of the polite imperative plural in Middle English.
    that is myn accord 'that is the agreement you made with me'.
842. *lat be youre shamefastnesse* 'never mind your shyness'.
843. *ley hond to* 'take hold of' your straw.
844. *anon to drawen every wight bigan* 'at once everyone drew'.
846. *by aventure, or sort, or cas* 'by some kind of chance'. The
distinction between the different terms is not important.
847. *the cut fil to the Knight* 'the deciding straw went to the
Knight': whether the longest or the shortest is uncertain.
850. *by foreward and by composicioun* 'according to our
agreement'.
853. *obedient* 'compliant, submissive'.
856. *A Goddes name* 'in God's name'.
859. *right a mirie cheere* 'a cheerful expression'.

GLOSSARY

accord agreement
achaat purchase
achatours caterers
acordaunt to in accordance with
acorded (l. 244) suited, befitted; (l. 820) agreed
adrad afraid
aferd frightened
affile make smooth
again against
al entirely
al be although
alderbest best of all
ale-stake sign outside a tavern
algate in either case
alight dismounted
aller (l. 588) all (of them); (l. 825) all (of us)
als as
amblere ambling-horse
amorwe in the morning
anlaas two-edged dagger
anon immediately
apes fools
apiked decorated
areste stop
arette impute, ascribe
aright exactly, just like
array dress, state
arrerage arrears
arwes arrows
ascendent ascendant; degree of the ecliptic rising at a given time
asonder apart
assoilling absolution

astored provided
atones at the same time
avaunce benefit, bring profit
avaunt assurance, boast
aventure chance, coincidence
avys consideration
ay always
baar bore, carried
balled bald
bar carried
baren behaved
barge sailing-ship
bawdrik baldric, belt
been be
beggestere beggar
ben be
bereth conducts, behaves
bet better
bifalle happened
bifil it happened
biforn before
bigan did; began
bigonne taken precedence
bisette employed, applied
biside outside, near
bisily earnestly
bismotered marked, stained
bit commanded
bithoght considered, thought of
blankmanger see note, l. 389
bokeler buckler, small round shield
boote remedy
boras borax
bord table
born borne, behaved

129

bracer wrist-guard, used by archers

brawn muscles

breem bream, a lake fish

bretful brimful

brode broad, plain-spoken

broille broil, grill

brood broad

burdoun ground melody

caas (l. 325) legal case; (l. 799) affair

cake loaf of bread

carf carved

carl churl, common fellow

carpe talk, chat

cas accident

catel property

caughte seized upon

ceint girdle

ceruce white lead

chaped mounted

chapeleyne secretary, assistant

chapman merchant

charitable tender-hearted, kindly

chaunterie chantry (see note, l. 512)

cheere appearance, behaviour

cherubinnes cherub's

chevissaunce money-dealings

chiere welcome, greeting

chiknes chickens

chivachie cavalry campaigning

clasped fastened

cleped called

clepen call

clerk scholar

cloisterer monk

cofre money-chest

colerik choleric (see note, l. 589)

colpon strip, thin cluster

compeer familiar friend

complexioun temperament

composicioun agreement, arrangement

concubyn mistress

condicioun state, circumstance

conscience (ll. 142, 150) tender feeling, sensibility; (ll. 400, 528) moral consciousness

conseil private secrets, counsel

cop top

cope cape

coppe cup

corage nature, desire, ardour

cordial medicine which invigorates the heart

cosin related to

countour auditor

countrefete imitate

courtepy short coat

covenant legal agreement

covered prepared for a meal

covine deceitfulness

craft skill

crike creek, inlet

crois cross

crulle curly

curat parish priest

cure care, diligence

curious (l. 196) skilfully made; (l. 579) erudite

curs sentence of excommunication

cursen excommunicate

cursing excommunicating

curteis courteous, of gentle behaviour

curteisie courtesy, good manners

daliaunce chat, flirtation, love-making

Glossary

daunger (l. 404) peril; (l. 665) power
daungerous imperious, arrogant
dayerie dairy
dayeseie daisy
deed dead
degree social rank
deis dais, raised platform
delivere agile
delve dig
desdeyn disdain, contempt
despitous scornful, spiteful
desport amusement, mirth
dettelees out of debt
devis will, direction
devise relate, describe
deyntee (adj.) fine, superior; (sb.) delicacy
digne (l. 141) worthy; (l. 518) disdainful
dike make ditches
dischevelee dishevelled, with disordered hair
discreet judicious
dispence spending
disport diversion, amusement
dokked docked, cut short
doomes legal judgements
doon do
dong manure
dormant permanent
dorste dared
doumb dumb
draughte amount drunk at one 'pull'
dresse set in order
drogges drugs
droghte drought, period without rain
duszeyne dozen
ecclesiaste ecclesiastic, divine
echon each one

eek also
ellis else
embrouded embroidered
encombred endangered
encrees increase
endite (l. 95) write verses; (l. 327) draw up documents
engendred (l. 4) generated; (l. 423) were produced
enoint anointed
ensample example
entuned intoned
envined stocked with wine
er before
ercedekenes archdeacon's
eris ears
erst before
eschaunge exchange (of currency)
ese pleasure
esed made comfortable
estatlich, estatly dignified, stately
everemoore always, continually
everich each one, every
everichoon every one
everydeel every bit, altogether
eyen eyes
facultee profession, official position
fader father
fain willingly
fairnesse gentle means
falding coarse woollen cloth
famulier familiar, intimate
farsed stuffed, stuck
faste close, near
felawe low-class fellow, friend
felaweshipe fellowship, company

fer far
ferme rent
ferne far-off
ferre further
ferrer further
ferreste most distant
festne fasten
fet brought
fetis neat, graceful, well-made
fetisly elegantly, gracefully
feyne invent
figure saying
fil, fille fell
finch small bird; allusively a dupe
fiithele fiddle
Flaundrissh from Flanders
flex flax
flour-de-lys fleur de lis, lily-flower
floytinge playing the flute
folwed followed
fond found
foo enemy
foreward, forward agreement, promise
forneys furnace
forpined wasted by suffering
forster forester
fortunen choose favourable combination of astrological influences
foryeve forgive
fother load
frankeleyne franklin
fredom nobility, generosity
frere friar
ful very
fulle, atte completely
fustian thick cotton cloth
fyn fine
fyr fire

gadrede gathered
galingale flavouring substance obtained from an Indian plant
gamed pleased
gat-tothed gap-toothed
geere (l. 354) utensils; (l. 367) equipment
gentil well-bred, charming, worthy
gerner garner
geten obtained
ginglen jingle
gipon tunic worn under the hauberk
gipser purse, pouch
girles youths of both sexes
girt belted
gise manner, method
glaringe glistening, staring
gobet fragment
goliardeys jester, buffoon
good property
goodly kindly
goon go
goot goat
governaunce rule, care, control
governour leader
gretteste biggest, most considerable
greyn grain
gris costly grey fur
grope examine
ground texture
grounded well instructed
habergeon hauberk, coat of mail
halve half
halwes shrines
han have
hardily certainly
harlot rascal, low fellow

harlotries obscene and scurrilous tales
harneised accoutred, mounted
harre hinge
haunt skill
heeng hung
heep lot, crowd
heigh high
helpen heal, cure
hem them
heng, -e hung
hente take, took
herberwe (l. 405) harbour, anchorage; (l. 767) inn, lodging
heris hairs, bristles
hethenesse heathendom
hewe complexion
hider hither
hierde herdsman, shepherd
highte was called
himselven himself
hindreste last, hindermost
hine farm labourer
hir their
hire her
holden held, considered
holpen cured
holt copse
holwe hollow, hungry
hoole whole
hoolly entirely
hoom home
hoomly informally
hoote hot
hosen stockings
hostiler innkeeper
humour see note, l. 422
hy lofty
ilke same
infect invalidated
inspired quickened, breathed upon

janglere rowdy babbler
jet fashion, mode.
jolitee sport, bravado
juste joust, tourney
kan know, be able
keep heed
kept protected
knarre sturdy fellow
koude knew how to, could
kouthe could manage
kowthe known, familiar
laas lace, cord
large broad, free-spoken
late recently, newly
latoun latten, a compound of zinc and copper
lazar leper
lecherous lascivious
leed cauldron
leet (ll. 128, 175) let, allowed; (l. 510) left, abandoned
lene lend
lest desire, pleasure
leste desired, wished
letuaries electuaries, remedies
levere rather
lewed ignorant, untaught
licour juice, moisture
likned til comparable to
limitour see note, l. 209
lipsed lisped
liste wished
litarge protoxide of lead
liveree livery, distinctive dress
lode-menage navigation
loore teaching
looth reluctant
lordinges sirs, gentlemen
lough low
love-dayes days for settling disputes
lovyere lover

luce pike
lust pleasure, delight
lusty joyous, vigorous
lyk like
maistrie mastery, control
male baggage
maner kind of
marybones marrow-bones
medlee medley, cloth of mixed
  weave
meede (l. 82) meadow; (l. 772)
  reward
mercenarie person working
  only for money
meschief misfortune
mesurable moderate,
  temperate
mete, at at table
miscarie come to harm
mo more
mormal purulent sore
mortreux thick soup or stew
morwe morning
moste must
mote may
mottelee motley, particoloured
  cloth
muche and lite high and low
muchel much
murierly more merrily
muwe coop, pen
mury, murye, myrie merry,
  glad, pleasant
myster trade, occupation
namo no more, no other
narwe narrow
nas was not
nathelees none the less
neet cattle
nice scrupulous
nightertale night-time
noght not, not at all

nolde would not
nones, for the (l. 381) for the
  occasion; (l. 525) at once;
  (l. 547) indeed
noon no, none
noot don't know
norissing nutriment,
  sustenance
nosethirles nostrils
not heed head with close-
  cropped hair
nowthe, as at present
ny close
o one
offertorie anthem sung while
  the offering is collected
offring gifts made to priest by
  his parishioners
oinement ointment
oon, after uniformly good
ooth oath
ounces small gatherings
outrely absolutely,
  completely
outridere monk who rode out
  to inspect monastic estates
overeste upper
overspradde spread over
owher anywhere
paas walking pace
pace (l. 36) proceed; (l. 175)
  pass away; (l. 576) excel,
  surpass
palfrey riding-horse
pardee par dieu; by God,
  certainly
parfit perfect
parisshens parishioners
passed excelled
patente letter-patent, licence
  of appointment
pees peace

134

peire set, string
perced penetrated
per chaunce probably, doubtless
pers blue-grey cloth
person, persoun parson, priest
peyned took pains, endeavoured
phisik medicine
piled straggly
pilwe-beer pillow-case
pinche at find fault with
pinched pleated, fluted
pitaunce gift
pitous compassionate
plentevous abundant
pleyen chaff, banter
pleyn complete, absolute
pomely dappled
poraille poor people
port bearing, demeanour, manner
poudre-marchant powder-merchant, a sharp flavouring material
poure pore, gaze intently
povre penniless
poynaunt pungent
praktisour practitioner
prikasour mounted huntsman
priking spurring; tracking hares
prively secretly
propre personal, own
prys (l. 237) prize; (l. 817) price
pulle pluck
pulled plucked, drawn
pultrie poultry
purchas (verb) gain, acquire; (sb.) takings, gains
purchasour buyer of land

purfiled trimmed at the edges
purtreye draw
quite requite, reward
rage frolic
raughte reached
recchelees irresponsible, unmindful of duty
reed (adj.) red; (sb.) adviser
reherce repeat
remenaunt remainder, rest
renning charging
rente income
reportour arbiter
reule rule, order
reuled guided, governed
reverence respect
reysed made raids
right just
roialliche royally, ceremoniously
rood rode
roost roasted meat
rote small stringed instrument
rote, by by heart
rouncy carthorse
rounded fell in a round shape
route company, band
rudeliche bluntly, coarsely
sangwin (l. 335) sanguine (see note, l. 335); (l. 441) scarlet cloth
saucefleem having pimples or eruptions
saugh saw
sautrie psaltery; a stringed instrument played by plucking
scalled scabby
scarsly frugally
scathe pity
science knowledge
sclendre slender

scole school
scoleye study
seche seek
seeke sick
seigh saw
seken seek, search for
semely comely, becomingly, pleasingly
semicope short cope or cape
sendal thin silk
sentence serious meaning
servisable willing to serve
sethe boil
seyl sail
shamefastnesse modesty
shape prepare
shapen intend
shaply likely, suitable
sheeldes French *écus*, coins
sheene shiny
shine shin
shirreve sheriff
shiten defiled
sho shoe
shorte with make short
short-sholdred square-bodied
sike diseased
sikerly certainly, truly
sin since
sithes, ofte oftimes
slee kill
sleighte cunning, craftiness
smerte (adv.) sharply, painfully; (verb) cause pain, suffer
smothe smooth
snewed snowed
snibben rebuke, admonish
sobrely gravely
solaas amusement, entertainment
solempne dignified, impressive

somdel somewhat
sondry various
soong sang
soore sorely, painfully
soote sweet
soothly truly
soper supper
sort lot
sothe truth
soun noise
souple pliant, flexible
sovereyn chief, principal
sowne play upon
sowninge (l. 277) proclaiming; (l. 309) tending towards
space, the meanwhile
spak pronounced
spare refrain, cease
sparwe sparrow
speede prosper
spores spurs
springe dawn
stepe large, protruding
sterres stars
stif bold, strong
stiwardes stewards
stonden stand, remain in
stoor stock
stot stallion
stout strong
streit strict
streite tightly
strem river
strike hank, bunch
strondes shores
stuwe fish-pond
substaunce possessions
subtilly subtly, cleverly
suffisaunce sufficiency, contentment
surcote outer coat
swerd sword

swich such

swink (sub.) labour, work

swinken (verb) labour, work

swinkere labourer

swyn swine

taille, by on account

takel weapons, equipment

talen tell stories

tapicer weaver of tapestry

tappestere barmaid

targe shield

taryinge delay

termes phrases, expressions

termes, in exactly

than, thanne then

ther as there, where

therto in addition

thilke that same

tho those

thries three times

thriftily efficiently

tipet tippet, cape

toft tuft

togidre together

tollen take toll

tretis graceful, well-formed

trompe trumpet

trowe believe, think

tukked having his coat tucked into his belt

tweye two

twinne depart, separate

undergrowe under-developed

undertake warrant, declare

usage habits and customs

vavasour substantial landholder

venerie hunting

vernicle reproduction of St Veronica's handkerchief

verraily truly

verray true, real, exact

viage journey

vigilies vigils; meetings or services on the eve of holy days

vileynie (l. 70) harm, wrong; (l. 728) coarse and churlish behaviour or speech

vitaille victuals, provisions

voirdit verdict

vouche sauf grant, permit

walet wallet

wan earned

wandringe travelling

wantowne gay, unruly, lascivious

wantownesse affectation

war (adj.) cautious, discreet; (verb) guard against

war, was observed

wastel-breed fine white bread

wateringe watering-place

waterlees out of water

webbe webster

weel well

wende go

wered wore

weren were

werken act, do

werre war

werte wart

weyeden weighed

wex wax

whan that when

whelkes pimples, blotches

whilom once, formerly

whil that while

widwe widow

wif middle-class woman

wight person, creature

wimpul wimple (see note on l. 472)

winne earn money

Glossary

winning profits, earnings
wiste knew
wit brains, ingenuity
withalle therewith, moreover
withholde engaged for service
withseye deny, refuse
wolden would, wished to
wonder remarkably
wone habit
wood mad
woning dwelling
woot know
worstede worsted, type of woollen cloth
write written, inscribed
wroght (l. 369) made; (l. 499) took action
wrooth angry
wyd spacious, extensive
wyn wine
wys wise
ybore carried
ycleped called
ydrawe drawn

yfalle fallen
yknowe diagnosed
ylad led
ylik like
ypreved proved
yronne run
ysene visible, to be seen
yshadwed shaded, screened
yshorn cut
yshrive absolved
yteyd tied
ywimpled see note, l. 472
ywroght made
yaf gave
ye eye
yeddinges ballads, songs
yeldehalle gildhall
yeldinge yield
yeman yeoman; servant or attendant
yemanly in yeomanly fashion
yerde stick, rod
yeve, yeven give
yive give